A Hiding Place
From
The Wind

To Jack & Laura

Dorinda Lundin

Dorinda K. D. Lundin

Editing Services - Alison Downs

Cover Art- Beverly Anderson Jaken
Original Oil on Wood - from a historical photograph of the "Hiding Place"

ISBN – 13:9781537759036

2016

Printed by CreateSpace

Dedication

Elna Sophia Johnson
April 19, 1915 - November 16, 1931

Life is a wind that blows both fair and foul but blow it will…

Contents

A Hiding Place
From
The Wind

Prologue

To say that I met my family in May when pear blossoms perfumed the air and that we fell in love immediately would perhaps be more romantic, but we did not. We met in the harsh of December amid the sleet and frozen rain of an early Connecticut winter. I was new and fresh, the hope of the future, the first of the next generation. They, my extended family, were the goers of the past, the risk takers, the builders and the imaginers, but life is a wind that blows both fair and foul, but blow it will and each of us must find our way.

In the spring of 1920 my grandparents acquired a small subsistence farm in rural northeastern Connecticut. Here among the rolling hills with its patchwork of forests and fields, its gurgling streams and sparkling lakes, my grandparent's countrymen had discovered a region that looked and felt much like their beloved homeland but offered opportunity—a commodity of short supply in turn-of-the-century Scandinavia. The region enticed these newcomers, each with a story and each with a unique dream.

For many the dream was to farm the hills and valleys, to control their destiny, to own a piece of earth. Land and a farm, that was real wealth, something to be passed on to one's sons. The English had been the first to put plow to this boney New England soil. They birthed the villages and towns, axed the forests for farms... but try as they might, the boney soil conquered even the hardiest of pioneer farmers. One by one the farms grew fallow and faltered. To the Scandinavian immigrants, however, the soil was kinder than the land they left behind. They knew by birth how to make these reluctant lands blossom and bloom, and they did. The struggle was no easier here than it had been in the old country, but what they toiled for now belonged to them, every stubborn rock, every tillable furrow of soil and every harvest, plentiful or meager, it was theirs. It made the laborious work of farming worthwhile.

My grandparents shared a heritage with their neighbors, but they were neither pioneer immigrants nor farmers; Grandfather's family had come to America to escape that life. As a result, my grandfather—born just days after his family arrived in New York—became a trained and gifted architect. The only life he knew was one of business, construction, and religion. My grandmother, older than my grandfather, had been a youthful immigrant to America. She had lived her childhood in a kinder Sweden than Grandfather's family had known and her memories of those years had been overwritten by a rich and diverse American experience. The young couple began their life together in an urban setting. As their family grew, it was the metronome of turn-of-the-century New York that metered their lives, one that had become moderately comfortable and secure.

But life is a wind that blows both fair and foul, but blow it will.

Life's flow is seldom constant. Sometimes it changes slowly, its movement barely noticeable but in one unsuspecting moment that flow can wheel about and abruptly re-channel the course of life. Whatever its cadence, nothing is as constant as change.

For my grandparents, that change came with the birth of their fourth child. Born in the spring of 1915, it was soon evident that the infant was suffering from a mysterious condition. The child was not even six months old when the convulsions and seizures began, then persisted as she grew. At first, doctors were unwilling to commit to a diagnosis and initially labeled her as suffering from a condition that they called *bubbles on the brain*, but what were those bubbles? Was she epileptic and suffering from seizures common to the disease, or were these seizures only one manifestation of a more complex condition? What sinister complications were silently at work within the child's body?

My grandparents' home in Corona, New York was within sight of the Tiffany Furnace. This factory was the production center for the unique and highly coveted Tiffany glass. Prized for its art, décor and architectural applications, the products of this industrial icon achieved production highs during the years my family lived within its shadow. The entire neighborhood, including my grandparents' home was subjected to an array of heavy metals and chemicals. Each day the factory wastes and by-products were dispensed into the environment: dissolved into the water, borne upon the air, and left as residue stagnating in the soil.

Tiffany glass became symbolic as the optimum expression of beauty and elegance, yet hidden just below its magnificence was a crouching monster waiting to pounce upon the unexpected. Within reach of those poisonous claws were the children: some unborn, some in the formative years of development, and perhaps some harboring life-altering changes within their genetic code. Those changes could remain dormant and hidden for years, waiting to surface in unsuspecting generations yet to be born. Was my aunt's condition epilepsy or perhaps poisoning from the commonly used lead and other heavy metals? Was her condition the simmering of a complicated soup of medical or mental conditions? Perhaps it was even an early case of the yet unknown scourge of autism?

At the time my aunt was born, the laws of New York State authorized institutionalized incarceration of the mentally insane. Sufferers of epilepsy and other unknown mental afflictions were still considered lunatics and thus insane. If my aunt's seizures and her retarded mental growth became serious enough to draw unwanted attention to her problems, the family risked social ostracism and serious legal action. While there was a growing recognition within medical circles that epilepsy was a condition apart from insanity and that treatments were being developed and tried with trial populations, any real advancement for the condition was meager at best. All too often any new treatment was quickly rejected in favor of the fear-driven historical treatment method: remove the afflicted from society, lock them away from sight, sterilize them and dehumanize them. It was a plan to protect the many from the few.

Stories are written about the famous and the heroic. My family was not famous but they were heroic in the way that they refused to succumb to the customary opinions of the day. Instead they believed that their daughter, though different from the rest of their family, was nothing less than a unique, beautiful person and a member of their family. They vowed to preserve their family unit, to keep it whole and intact. Such opinions were unique in the early 1900s as fear more often dictated a family's reaction to such adversity. Because of her differences and the fear surrounding her illness, people like my aunt were more often shunned than embraced.

The trials my grandparents faced were difficult, real, and uncannily similar to the challenges confronting all families of disabled children even today a hundred years later. And like today, the early 1900s was a complex time, with rapidly evolving technology and social thinking, political complications and shadows of war. As my grandparents struggled to cope, their predictable way of life was becoming a fearful future.

A Hiding Place From The Wind is a fictionalized account of a family's life with a disabled child. Set at the turn of the 20th Century, the story is firmly rooted in my family's experiences and how they lived their life through these difficult times. The characters in this story are not purely biographical, but instead the story is seeded with real characters and events that have grown through fictional license to embrace a larger story. Through the voice of my fictional characters, I hope to share a tale that my family could never have revealed in their own time.

In many ways my characters, like my family, are traditionalists, people who might have gone unnoticed for their entire life. They accepted that their religious convictions formed a matrix for their life, gave it meaning and form. They generally saw value in using the economic and governmental systems in place to achieve and move forward. They were not activists or revolutionaries and while not poor or uneducated, they struggled to be the proud American middle class family of their time and passionately embraced education as the ladder to success.

All of that changed in a moment of realization, the day the convulsions began. It was on that day that they ceased to be *just like all the others*, it was the day life forced them to fight for what they loved and cared about. From that day forward even the simplest of life's activities took on an added dimension of accommodation, frustration, and despair. It might have been easier for them had my aunt been institutionalized, but that was never a consideration. For this family the "winds of life" had begun a constant travail of change.

A Hiding Place From The Wind

Part One: The Winds

Southern Sweden
1891

Ancient tombstones, some whose posture beckoned an impending topple, ringed all sides of the ancient stone church, save for a well-worn pathway that led to the *kyrka's* door. Perched high upon the only rise of high land, the small white church could be seen for miles. Though its bell tower was not especially high, one could view from the tower's small open window the land below, outstretched in all directions, flat like an opened hand until its fingertips touched the sky. In the season of growth, that prairie became a sea of bending and waving green. As the days lengthened and warmed, the greening morphed into a quilt of wildflower whites and reds and ended its colorful chameleon-like changes with a rush of mustard yellow blossoms that carpeted the landscape and rolled to the edge of the radiant blue sky. But the season of growth and harvest had now waned and the rainbow of color was gone, replaced by barren land that lay bristle brown and lifeless. Only a tiny village and a handful of manor houses with their umbilically tied farms were visible beyond the churchyard.

Today the cold blustery winds and sullen gray sky harbingered the approaching season of dormancy, of cold and of death. Windy gusts ripped at Kersti's shawl and smarted her face with cold, raw slaps, but today, the cruel winds cursed everyone. They tormented the old, the young, and each mourner that ringed the open grave.

Carefully the young woman picked her way along the rock and root strewn trail. Instinctively she chose her way despite the fact that her mind was awash with emotions, fears and uncertainty. Words of fear screamed at her sensibilities. *Is there ever a right time to bury your mother? One must be strong, Father says, but I am so very weak. Inside I quiver and shake. I'm so empty and alone. I want to cry but I can't, and even if I could, it isn't allowed where others can see such weakness. I ache for the darkness of night.* Amid the storm of emotions, the young woman, perhaps old for her years, was forced to angrily admit: for some things there is never a right time.

Her mother's sickness had come without warning. The condition never improved, it only stayed the same or worsened until all hope for a recovery was lost. Her mother's care had fallen to Kersti, the oldest daughter left at home, though she was hardly more than a child herself. Her father was a good man, but he had aged in ways that prevented him from helping Kersti with her Mama's daily care. Yes, there were others, brothers and sisters, but their lives were no longer in the family's cottage; each had grown, left, and found their own life. So Kersti, the dutiful daughter, obeyed without question the orders of her Poppa and older siblings.

Her Mama had always been the strong one, the salve for everyone's ills, their storehouse of knowledge, their unfailing support, but now she was gone and today Kersti respectfully followed Poppa, her brothers and sisters, the priest, and her Mama's small wooden casket towards the open grave. The others carried the casket, but for Kersti, a deep seemingly unfillable emptiness weighted down her every footstep. Only her younger sister walked with her.

"What will happen to us now, Kersti? Will I stay with you? Where will Poppa go? Who's going to take care of Poppa? Where will we live?"

The child questioned out of fear, but Kersti had no answers.

The child, Emma, reached up and grasped her sister's hand, entwining her fingers through hers as if seeking protection from the scene around them. Instinctively, Kersti pulled the tiny girl closer to her side and there they stood, clutching each other in stoic silence as the parish priest chanted the litany of burial and entreated the Lord to be merciful to the departed who was about to be lowered into the cold, unforgiving earth.

On an eerily similar gray morning, half a lifetime ago, Kersti had first experienced death. She had stood in this same churchyard, wound tightly into the folds of her mother's skirt so that she would not have to watch as her sister was laid to rest. She remembered hearing the dull thuds of the soil as shovelful after shovelful of the heavy, dark earth fell hard against the coffin, but mostly she remembered feeling her mother's silent sobs. It scared her, those cries that made no sound, the pain that throbbed within but remained silenced.

The task finished, each mourner turned and retraced their footsteps, but Kersti lingered for just one more precious moment. It was in this moment that the priest, a man who had served their village for decades, reached down and lifted a small prayer book from the casket's lid. He turned to Kersti. "Let this help you with your life, my child. Let it guide you and help you. Your Mama, she was a good woman."

The priest's soft words of condolence surprised her. His hand pressed the small, supple book into hers. Somehow, as if by providence, he knew what burdens lay beyond today.

Life is a wind that blows both fair and foul, but blow it will.

No Time For Fear
Corona, New York
1915

Morning's first light crept across the small bedroom windowsill, then, like an intruder intent upon banishing the night, it flashed tiny spotlight glows of golden onto the colorful papered walls of the nursery. The soft light inched across the walls until it found the face of a sleeping woman and bathed her skin with golden warmth. Her eyes opened to blinding sunlight.

Instantaneously, Kristine was awake.

Where am I? Why am I here? Had I fallen asleep? How long have I been sleeping? Confusion flooded her mind. *Where is my daughter? Little Sophie? Is she all right? Had there been another seizure? Had she choked? Was she still alive?*

The young mother struggled to gain control of the moment and still the pounding that threatened to explode from within her chest. Her hands groped the bedclothes for the form of her tiny daughter, stopping only when her fingers discovered the rhythmic motion of the swaddled child's breathing.

She's fine, just sleeping, she realized, but her hand lingered as the soothing movement of Sophie's sleeping body pacified her panic.

To the family she was simply known as Mama, a warm and endearing term, but to most others she was now Kristine. Some years ago she had chosen to Americanize her Swedish birth name. Kersti was who she had been and she involuntarily bristled at its use. The emotions and images it wrested up were from a time she'd mostly prefer to forget. No, she was in America now and this was the future. Kristine was her American name and it made her feel proud.

Kristine's night vigil was ending, but even as the tiny room brightened, even as life noises began to fill the farthest reaches of the house and the routines of the morning began, she remained seated in the child's nursery. Out of habit, her hand reached towards the small prayer book on the lamp stand. Her fingers caressing its worn cover, but the missal remained unopened. *Let this help you with your life* the priest of the Kersti years had said, words spoken to comfort and still the fears of the unknown. Kristine lifted the tiny book from its rest upon the table and held it tightly to her chest, but knew no prayer under its cover could ease her fears or soothe her silent cries of pain.

It had been her habit to begin and end her days with the prayers within the small book's covers, but of late she was ashamed to admit the prayers had become little more than lamentations. At times her words were mere whispers or wandering, like now in her daughter's room at morning's first light. But after all her family was safely asleep and Kristine was alone with the darkness of night, before her weary body accepted the reluctant pleas for sleep, her fears found words and those words pleaded for help that did not come.

Kristine's prayers always began the same: *Oh, Lord, Am I going mad? What is happening to my little Sophie? I don't understand, Lord, I don't understand. It must be madness, but is it my madness or is it my child's? Lord, why would you cause such a beautiful, innocent child to suffer so? Why? What have we done, what have I done to cause this pain to the innocent?*

She felt the words catch in her throat. *Why can't others see what's happening to the child? The doctor, even dear Poppa, why can't they see her struggle? Can it be that I alone can feel her agony and suffering? I love her, I feel her pain and I cannot help her. Please help her Lord; please oh please help me too, for I no longer know what to do.*

Kristine could not continue. Images of the child's writhing body flooded her memory and moments of anguish from the child's last spell replayed endless in her mind. Once again, as vivid as the moment it first occurred, the young mother felt the panic of the convulsive attack and fear rose within her as the memory invaded every fiber of her body. She watched again as her daughter's soft brown eyes transformed to a steely cold stare into the unknown. The child's body jerked, twisted, contorted and became rigid; her beautiful brown eyes rolled upward and away, leaving only cold white orbs within their sockets. Milky foam spewed from Sophie's lips. The moment became an intolerable eternity while the unresponsive child lay bathed in her own bodily fluids, her soft ivory skin now a perverted ashen gray. Then, almost as quickly as the seizure had begun, it ended. The child's rigid body became limp; a natural color slowly refilled her countenance and the soft brown color of her eyes returned, but within minutes they had closed again, this time in a deep restorative sleep.

* * * * * * *

Soon after the child was born, Kristine knew something was different. All the other children, three before Sophie, had all experienced their moments of fussiness, colic, and other normal childhood difficulties, but Sophie's condition continued to worsen. When the spells and fits began, she had confided in Rob, but these different moments never seemed to happen when he was at home.

"She's just an extra fussy baby, Kristine. I'm sure she'll grow out of this condition."

"Rob, if you don't call the doctor to come to Sophie, I'll find a way to bring her to his office myself," she demanded of her husband on one especially trying day. Kristine's desperation had reached a breaking point. That fact was clearly evident, so this time, though he disagreed with her about the seriousness of the situation, there was no argument.

"I'll take care of it," he said, "and somehow the Lord will provide us with the money to pay for the visit."

It's so easy to avoid believing that something could be wrong, that the problem will go away and all will be better tomorrow. It's easier and safer to explain away something that one doesn't want to see.

Kristine wished she could tell Poppa how she really felt, but this she realized she must keep to herself, at least for now. Nor did it help that just as Rob had predicted, the doctor found nothing in particular wrong with Sophie. So after the doctor's visit Kristine kept quiet about Sophie's difficulties, sharing her fears only in letters home to her sister and in her pleas to the Lord.

The incidents continued. Sometimes they were so mild that only Kristine's sensitive eye saw the moment of Sophie's detachment, but often they were severe and frightening. After one dangerous episode, it was Rob who insisted on calling the doctor to come and examine her once again. After a thorough check up, he could offer little help.

"Croup can cause this," the doctor concluded. So he gave Kristine some evil-smelling syrup for congestion and left with the promise to come back in a week, but in a week the child was no better.

Kristine's Attitude

Talking to just anyone about personal things, like her fears or her daughter's condition, didn't fit Kristine's personality; those matters she believed one kept to oneself. If you did share such thoughts, it was only with one's must trusted personal confidant. How she wished her sister hadn't returned to Sweden. While Emma had been in America, the two sisters had grown close to each other, even closer than in those dark and difficult days following their Mama's death. Kristine had found a real friend in her sister, someone that was special, an intimate fellow dreamer. She had paid for Emma's passage to New York. Both single and skilled in domestic service, they carried themselves with an aristocratic air that ensured prime employment would quickly be secured. The sisters had experienced this provincial land together, both had eaten from the bounty of its table, and dreamed of finding that one special person with whom to make a life and home of their own. But Emma was gone now, lured home by her first true love, married and with her own growing family. In these dark days when she needed her sister the most, Kristine could only pen her fears and heartache in letters that took weeks to find a reader. The separation bore heavily on her, especially now, when she felt she had no one to turn to, no one just for her.

Kristine wished Rob could be a special friend and confidant too, but their marriage was the result of a common sense arrangement by Rob's father. They were friends, to be sure, and had been for many years. The bond between them was growing stronger with time and each conflict weathered, but now in these seminal years of their union, Rob's allegiance was primarily to his role as the son of an eminent church leader, to their other children's well being and to his professional occupation. Kristine had a role, too; it was to be her husband's helpmate. In that role she supported her young husband in all he was called to do, created and maintained a well-appointed home, and raised the children according to the dictates of their lives. Nowhere had the rules of marriage called upon the couple to share their innermost emotions. It was just how it was, those unwritten rules of life.

Kristine was not an unlikeable young woman, quite the opposite in fact. In her role of choice she was affable and easily liked, but these acquaintances and "friends" were all part of her life as Rob's wife. They were the church ladies of the Mission Aid Society and Anthem Choir. They were the women and occasional men who gathered in Rob and Kristine's parlor for church meetings or midweek prayer services, and they came because of Rob and his role within his father's fledging church. For the most part they were all good people, albeit a bit pious on occasion, but they were not her confidants or close special friends. That role belonged exclusively to her sister and a few choice individuals.

No matter what the occasion or gathering, it always was the same group of women who entered Kristine's parlor. They were sober, pious, and punctual, all arriving within moments of each other. Kristine loved fashion, color, and well-crafted garments, but all the worshippers seemed to be cut from the same bolt of cloth, gray homespun. The garments were gathered tightly about their corset and hung lifelessly to the floor. Their hair was similar too, all pulled back into a bun at the base of their neck and ornamentations, if they possessed any, had been carefully been left at home. They gathered and hung on every word of Rob's Bible discussions. They planned bazaars for the war effort, sewing projects for missions, and pageants and programs for every Sunday of the month. And they talked and talked and talked.

"Have those woman nothing better to do with their time than to chatter and flit their buzz of gossip?" Kristine remarked to Rob after one especially long evening. "Ugh," she murmured as she gathered the refreshment dishes, "they could at least have helped me bring the dishes into the kitchen. They just went on and on tonight. There is so much happening that's worth talking about, but I think I'll scream if I hear another word about Mrs. Iverson's aches and pains."

Kristine wasn't a gossiper, a skill she learned early on in her American life. "I must be able to trust you completely," her prestigious employer Mrs. Robbson had once told her. "To be a good lady's maid you must be my secret ears and eyes. You will see and hear much that can never be repeated or shared with anyone except me."

Her employer's words proved to be prophetic. Kristine had just returned from accompanying Mr. and Mrs. Robbson on a European Grand Tour when scandalous rumors concerning the prominent couple began circulating in the newspapers. The drama worsened with accusations and counter attacks that produced vitriolic copy for the society pages of the *New York Times*. Finally the fatal punches connected and the couple divorced in a media sensation of its time. Mrs. Robbson was banished to live a pauper's life by the standards of the age, stripped of her name and position. But Kristine, who had lived within the household for almost 10 years, had known it all but never shared a word with anyone.

This life of learning through observation had come naturally to the young woman who had found listening of much greater value than talking. It's how she learned to read, write, and speak English, to prepare an elegant meal, to dress for success… but more importantly; she learned how to read people's intent. It was an approach to life she liked. It gave her an edge, but the church ladies all called it "Kristine's Attitude."

"I know what each of those women is thinking no matter what they are saying," she once told her oldest daughter Beth. "And then I watch their actions. They are often at crossed purposes. How they can call themselves Christians often causes a prickle down my spine. For me, it's easier to talk about almost anything else, Beth—the weather, a recipe from home or a sewing project—than to pass on their jabs and unkindness. Be careful, Beth, it is so easy to be drawn into their traps." If the talk did occasionally get a little too personal, and it did when events in the life of Sophie or the Johnson's household escaped to the public domain, Kristine would skillfully move their probing questions and comments far away from her family's personal affairs or her daughter's problems. After all, in the end, most people would rather tout their own accomplishments than those of others.

* * * * * * *

The days of Sophie's life inched along. Kristine tried to conceal her fears, but Poppa had learned to watch his daughter more intently.

"She's not improving very quickly is she, Kristine?" Rob's question jarred Kristine from her thoughts. She hadn't expected his interest. Perhaps she was beginning to scare him too.

"No Rob, she's not. She scares me, I don't know what do next."

Rob didn't say anything, but his eyes told Kristine all that she needed to know. He *was* scared, and like her he didn't know what to do either.

Rob, who often confided in his father, told Marten the intimate details of the child's most current problems, and Marten, in turn, told his wife. Now everyone seemed to know about the convulsions and how worried Kristine was about little Sophie. That was all that was needed for

Hanna, Kristine's mother-in-law and the midwife who delivered the child, to come by for a cup of coffee and a little talk.

"Kristine," she began, "the child will outgrow this. When I was a child I'm told that I had 'fits' like Sophie is having and look at me now, I have no problems. Even then, back home in the old country, it wasn't unusual for a child to have what were called epileptic fits. I've seen this in many of the children I delivered."

Hanna dunked her *skorpor* into the cup of dark coffee and ate the softened bread. "Oh, that was so good, Kristine. You are such a good cook, but such a worrier. With Sophie, it will pass. Don't listen too hard to the doctors, they don't know about children. You are worrying for nothing."

Well-intended words, Kristine thought to herself. *But that is not the answer.*

The child's seizures did not go away and after the most severe spell to date, Poppa arranged for yet another doctor's visit.

"Right now Mrs. Johnson," the doctor concluded, "the child seems fine. You say the fits are mostly at night, but I see nothing that has happened as a result of these episodes. I think you should bundle her up tightly and perhaps strap her in her bed so that she won't hurt herself. Keep her inside and don't expose her to crowds, as she is weaker than other children. There is too much sickness in this city right now. The influenza has become a terrible problem."

* * * * * * * *

The influenza pandemic, popularly called the Spanish Flu, was indeed a problem and the borough of Queens New York was its epicenter. The Marten Johansson's were a large, close-knit family. Rob, their first born in America, had six brothers but only one sister, Cecilia, born before Marten and Hanna sailed to America. Cecilia married young and bore her husband nine children before 1917, six of whom were still alive when she bore her newest, another son. It was a difficult time for Rob. He was troubled about his own daughter and her problems, but he also worried about his sister, the demands of her large family and now a newborn.

During her pregnancy Cecilia had not enjoyed the best of health. Her life was hard, demanding an intense effort to meet the needs of her husband and her large family. After the latest birth, she continued to struggle with her health. The doctor was called one morning when she failed to come down to prepare the morning meal.

"How long has she been so weak?" the doctor inquired of her husband.

"She was fine yesterday," her husband replied. "Just tired. The children, they require a lot. She was just tired."

"Did you know she'd been throwing up? It's called nausea and it dehydrates the body. See how her skin is changing color. That blue color means that today it's not just tiredness," the doctor paused. "Today it means she has the flu, the Spanish Flu. I'm sorry to tell you that by tomorrow or the next day she is likely to be dead."

The words were prophetic. Within one terrifying week the pandemic had struck with lightening speed. It claimed the lives of neighbors and friends and Rob's only sister Cecilia; the tragedy left a grief-stricken husband, his newest infant son and six other children of varying ages. Cecilia's oldest child, a daughter named Irma, would now become the surrogate mother for the brood.

For Rob and Kristine, who also grieved the loss of a pivotal family member, Cecilia's death had a rippling effect that directly affected them. The only extra help they had with Sophie had come from family members. Sometimes the help came from her mother-in-law Hanna, but most often it came from Irma, Cecilia's oldest child. It wasn't much, but it was help and it made things just a little easier. Cecilia's death changed all that. That help was now gone. The couple would have to find other solutions to their difficulties as the needs of others were greater and the family would have to rise to fill the void of a mother's death.

The Doctor's Surprise

The winds of winter had been cruel and everyone hoped that the soft breezes of spring would bring solace and peace. Spring quickly became summer then suddenly it was autumn, late autumn and almost two years had passed in Sophie's life. Today was special however, as it was the date of a long anticipated appointment with a special doctor. The trolley ride from Corona to the uptown New York doctor's office was agonizing—slow, wet, and cold. Once at the doctor's office the waiting was insufferable. It wasn't just the continual fussing of little Sophie or Poppa's restlessness or the crowded waiting room; it was a veil of fear that seemed to cling over everything, a veil that Kristine could no longer lift or cast aside. That foreboding had followed the trio here to this visit, to this examination room; one that she and Rob deeply hoped would provide some relief for their sense of helplessness and constant worry. Dr. Von Hess was a renowned doctor whose services they could never have sought, even in the best of times. Yet, here they were in his waiting room, the visit paid for by Rob's father Marten. They could repay the cost to him a little each month.

Kristine eyed in detail each and every movement of the doctor as he examined Sophie, their tiny Sophie so beautiful, so delicate and now so foreign. Each day the child had continued to change. Almost daily now her eyes would dull and her body stiffen and then suddenly she would collapse into that limp mass. Sophie was leaving them and going to a hiding place, a world of her own, where they could not follow. Would the day come when she would not return to them?

The doctor's voice called Kristine back to the present. "Mrs. Johnson, how long has she been exhibiting this behavior?"

Kristine's reserve kept her from answering immediately. The doctor repeated the question. "Since last September, Dr. Von Hess, I know, it was my birthday."

"Happy birthday." His voice was flat. "What happened that night? What was different?"

Rob answered the question. "The relatives, they came to give Kristine a surprise birthday party. She was feeding the baby in my office; it's quiet and away from the rest of the family. Kristine wasn't expecting it since her birthday had already passed, but all the family came in hooting and hollering and making a big deal of it, it being her 40th you see. It was a good time, and even though she was so very startled at their bursting in, by the end of the evening all seemed fine."

"The next day," Kristine continued as her courage returned, "Sophie just didn't act the same. She wouldn't nurse and she cried too much. Her eyes began to get a dull, cloudy look. I just knew something had happened. I blamed my milk! I blamed the surprise! I know—I poisoned my baby with fear, I just know it." Her voice cracked and she hesitated again as tears filled her eyes and the image of the evening overwhelmed and silenced her.

The doctor worked a bit longer with the child, and then turned to the couple.

"A long time ago, doctors would have drilled small holes in the skull to relieve the pressure on the brain and allow the dark humors to escape. Today we know that this can cause more problems than it solves. What I believe Sophie is suffering from is pressure on the brain and this is causing her convulsions. Epilepsy has been around for a long time and there are many causes, most of them unknown even now in 1917. My research and studies have caused me to theorize that the cause of this affliction is the result of some type of inflammation in the body, perhaps from substances the body has ingested or been exposed to and is now trying to rid itself of. I believe it's much like a splinter in a finger that pusses up, becomes inflamed and then is relieved when the pressure and splinter are removed. Something within Sophie's brain is producing pressures, much like bubble of a gas. I believe that these bubbles move around the brain and the convulsions are a result of the pressure on parts of the soft brain tissue. The convulsion resolves the problem for a short while. I believe most children do grow out of the seizures if they begin when the child is very young and there are few episodes, but Sophie's may not as she is older now and the seizures continue.

Today there are drugs—barbiturates and bromides, to name several—that are being given to some epileptics, but they have so many problems and I would not want to prescribe them for a child. There is not much we can do for your little girl. She will experience these epileptic seizures for most of her life, which may be shorter than your other children's lives. She must be watched carefully for she will be more of a threat to herself than she will be to others, but she will not grow and mature like your other children. A child with bubbles on the brain will be retarded in their development and learning. It will be a struggle for you and your family."

The trolley ride home was too long and too silent, the doctor's words replaying in both their minds, over and over again. His last words the harshest of all, ...*she may someday need to be committed to an institution for the feeble-minded.* It was like a pronouncement of death.

The Glass Pile

If you ran out the back door of the Johnson's Hunt Street house, scrambled down the rickety porch steps, bolted across the backyard past the tool shed and leaped over the little creek that separated adjoining backyards, you'd soon arrive at the glass pile. Equally well-worn paths led from neighboring yards to this treasure trove of coveted gems. Just beyond this mound of industrial rejects and waste products rose the brick walls of a building called the Tiffany Furnace.

The Tiffany Furnace was an industrial icon to the world, but to the children of the neighborhood it was a living, breathing alien beast. From deep within its belly, tongues of fire snapped and sparked while billows of smoke belched through its nostril smokestacks. Deep within that furnace, alchemist workers prepared secret formulas of precious metals and chemicals. Molten hot from the furnace, the glassworkers spun, blew, and rolled the precious glass into the world's most desired and beautiful glass art, the famed Tiffany Glass.

* * * * * * * * *

Slam, thump, thump, clomp, clomp! The quiet afternoon was suddenly alive with sound. The Johnson children were home from school.

"Beth! Close the front door! Willi, stop running! William, take those shoes off, now!"

"Yes Mama," the children's well-rehearsed answer echoed from the deep reaches of the upstairs bedrooms as they clamored to change from their only set of school clothes into a set of what they called play clothes. Minutes later, the energized trio reemerged, bounding straight towards the back door and the day's adventures.

"Children, come here, right now."

Mama always seemed to catch them just before they could escape the daily chores of the day. "Today, before you go play, I need your help."

Daily they tried to escape but seldom got beyond the porch before Mama's voice called then back into the kitchen. It was the harder part of family life; chores always awaited them before play. There was more work for them now that Mama had her hands full with Little Sophie and Dottie, their newest baby sister.

"Willi," Mama said, "today I want you to take Sophie with you to play. Put her on the blanket and keep an eye on her. She shouldn't go anywhere." Mama handed Willi a blanket for the ground and an old box that had totally absorbed Sophie's attention for much of the day.

"Yes, Mama." Willi suddenly felt limp and lifeless. Today she was planning to attack the glass mound in search of prizes for their neighborhood games and now she had to watch Little Sophie. There wasn't any use talking to Mama about this, when Mama told you to do something, you didn't argue.

"Come on, Sophie," Willi said, taking the child's hand and starting down the back steps, "we're going to the glass mound."

Sophie giggled and pulled at Willi's hand. "Fyer, Fyer." Sophie had started making her own language and Fyer was Willi's name. Well, at least she was happy today, Willi rationalized. Willi quickly found a grassy hillock near the scrap mound, plopped Sophie in the middle of her blanket and gave her sister the box. Sophie immediately began turning the box over to investigate every edge and side. She was intrigued with its colors and design. Willi was satisfied that the child was safe and quickly made a beeline for the mound of baubles which that day had attracted an unusually large crowd of neighborhood children. Word had quickly spread that workers had discarded a large amount of glass that morning. It was a great day for scrounging and time passed quickly.

"Hey Willi, your brat sister is bothering me." Willi looked up and Sophie wasn't on the blanket, she was at the edge of the mound and throwing tiny stones at Jonnie, one of the neighborhood bullies. Sophie didn't like Jonnie and she let him know the only way she knew how.

"What's the matter with her anyway?" Jonnie questioned. "She stupid or something?"

"She's fine. She's just a little kid."

"That's not what I hear. I hear she's sick, sick in the head," the bully taunted. "Sick in the head, she is, sick in the head."

Willi grabbed Sophie and pulled her back to her blanket and put the little box into her hand. The box had lost it fascination and she threw it to the ground. Willi sat down on the blanket and looked at her sister. "Sophie, what am I going to do with you?"

Not long ago, Mama had cautioned all the children to be especially careful when Sophie was outside. The days were growing warmer and everyone needed to be outside, including Sophie. "Sophie has an illness and you've all seen her spells, but other people might not understand her and get scared at what they see. There are some people who believe people who have an illness like Sophie's should be put into a special hospital because they fear what they don't understand. Poppa and I believe that one of these special hospitals wouldn't help your sister. She is part of our family and this is where she belongs, just like each of you. So try to keep Sophie safe and don't tell stories about her to others. She's your sister and part of our family."

With Mama's words fresh in her mind, Willi decided she should just sit with her sister for awhile, besides, now was a wonderful time to examine her glass pieces. She emptied her treasure bag onto the blanket and spread the glass pieces out to examine. Immediately, Sophie took an interest in the colorful glass objects, and just as promptly grabbed a colorful blue piece and popped it right into her mouth.

"Take that out right now," Willi grabbed at the piece of glass, but Sophie bit harder and shook her head. "No, spit that out! Bad girl!" Sophie ignored her.

All the activity was too much for little Sophie and suddenly her body stiffened and her eyes got a glassy look and rolled back into her head.

Willi panicked. "Oh no, Sophie is having a spell."

Willi had been with Sophie before when the spells came over her, but Mama had always been there, too. This time, however, she was on her own. The child's body tensed then began to jerk and foamy saliva flowed from her mouth that had finally released the light blue glass piece. It lay broken in two next to her head.

Willi was scared now, really scared, but Mama's words suddenly sounded as if they were right there in her head. *"Just be careful and hold her head lightly so she doesn't bang it against anything."* Willi pulled her sister closer to her and positioned her hands around her head.

"Good, just try to keep her on her side so the foam doesn't choke her." Willi did as she was instructed by that soft voice in her head. Gradually her sister seemed to be quieting. She stroked her hair and talked to her in soft tones trying to calm both of them. It seemed an eternity but gradually the child stilled, then relaxed as if she was about to fall asleep.

A gentle firm voice sounded behind her. "You did a really good job, Willi, now let's get her home to rest. Mama reached down and lifted the blanket and child into her strong arms.

"Mama?"

"Beth saw what was happening and ran to get me. Everything's fine now, Willi. You did all the right things. You were such a good sister. Let's all go home now."

Willi struggled to get up and then suddenly felt wet and cold. She looked down where her sister had laid next to her and a wave of embarrassment rushed over her and flushed onto her face. Sophie had peed and soiled the front of Willi's favorite gray play dress.

Sophie's Antics

Beth held her newest baby sister Dottie while Mama carefully changed the bedclothes on her crib. Tomorrow there would be more laundry to do and that thought irritated her. Of all the jobs Beth did for the family, laundry was the worst. A deep sigh escaped her lips and Mama heard it and almost as quickly sent her "look" towards Beth. Instantly, Kristine regretted her impulsive reaction. *She's a good girl and she's trying, we're all trying,* she thought to herself. *Perhaps only God knows how hard we're all trying.*

Kristine took the baby from Beth, laid her on the fresh bedclothes and tucked the child in for the night. Mama turned and looked at her oldest daughter.

"I think you've grown some more, Beth," she said. "You're becoming quite a young lady. Are you taller than William now?"

"Yes Mama, by almost a half an inch. Poppa said the same thing last night and measured us. He marked the doorpost this time. It's official." It was true; their family was growing up. Sophie was growing too and that was becoming a worrisome problem. Hardly a day passed when the words of Dr. Von Hess didn't echo in her mind; *Mrs. Johnson, your daughter must be watched carefully for she will become more of a threat to herself than to others.*

The child's problems were becoming more frequent and each a bit more unique. Each time Sophie became involved in a new situation, Mama could feel a knot of anticipation rise within her. No, not just anticipation that something would happen, it was a knot of fear that seemed to be with her all the time now. Where was that internal rest that she so longed for, those moments when she felt free of this growing stress that seemed to invade her entire being?

Not all of Sophie's antics proved to be problematic. Many of her antics were actually comical and wry in their innocence, however the latest did transgress into an area of family *correctness*. Lately, Sophie had taken to not wanting to wear clothes. Once Sophie was dressed for the day, she would take matters into her own hands. To Mama's dismay, a trail of discarded clothes would appear throughout the house. On one particular day, naked Sophie, with Mama in swift pursuit, streaked into Poppa's office as he sat working on a particularly difficult set of plans.

"Kristine, what is the meaning of this?" he thundered.

There were two things about Poppa that everyone in the family knew. First, you never disturbed Poppa while he was working and second, no one EVER ran around without his or her clothes on. He didn't even let the family wear bathrobes anywhere except from their bedrooms to the bathroom and everyone had to dress promptly before coming down for breakfast. After all, as the son of the church leader and superintendent of the Sunday school, Poppa's family had to set the example for others to follow. So, when Poppa dictated Mama was enlisted to enforce.

Luckily for everyone concerned, Sophie's natural phase was short lived. For a week the temperature dropped into the single numbers and stayed there. Cold invaded every crook and cranny of the Johnson's house. Keeping warm was a major job, so everyone put on extra layers of clothes and huddled together near the furnace vents, including Sophie. By the time the weather warmed, she'd forgotten about not wanting to wear clothes.

* * * * * * *

Usually Sophie was cheerful and cooperative, but sometimes her stubbornness worked against her—like the time Mama's neighborhood friend Gussie Schumann knocked frantically at the Johnson's front door.

"Kristine! Kristine! Do you know where Sophie is now? "

"She's upstairs in the bedroom, Gussie. Why do you ask?" Mama responded.

"No she's not! She's balance walking along the top of the roof railing. She'll fall Kristine! I just know she'll fall!"

Mama bolted up the stairs and sure enough, there was Sophie balanced and poised like a gymnast on the balcony railing two stories above the sidewalk. Mama went pale.

"Gussie," she shouted to her friend. "Get Rob. He's in his office…and find Willi if you can, Sophie listens to her. Hurry! Please hurry!"

Kristine sat down in front of the open window and softly called to her daughter.

"Sophie, Mama's here. Come inside now." Sophie looked at Mama and giggled.

"Sophie, can I come outside with you?"

The child turned and moved further along the roof railing. Mama slowly began to pull herself through the window onto the porch roof, but as she came closer Sophie inched further away from her.

Kristine kept talking to her in soft tones, saying nothing special, just talking, and soon Sophie was talking back to her in Sophie Talk which Kristine still didn't understand very well.

Gussie arrived with Rob and a ladder but no Willi. "Off playing with the neighbors or at the glass pile," she said. "Anyway, she's not going to be of any help to us."

"Kristine, move away from the window!" Rob shouted. "If I go up Sophie may want to get away from me and go back into the house through the window."

The cat and mouse game went as Poppa suggested and Sophie edged away from her father as he climbed the ladder. The bedroom window proved the best means of escape and she dutifully crept back into the house.

The next day, after the children had left for school, Kristine called Rob back into the kitchen for an extra cup of coffee, a piece of his favorite bread, and some private talk about Sophie.

"Rob," she began, "Sophie does things with no understanding of what will happen to her. She's intelligent, and that curiosity, it's something all our children seem to have in abundance, but for Sophie there is a difference. The other children learn from their mistakes, remember what happens to them, and then use that knowledge the next time. Sophie doesn't seem to be able to do that. For her, curiosity is often an enemy. It leads her to trouble."

"I've noticed that too. Kristine, what can we do? We can't be with her every moment of the day, there's just too much to do. This time she could have been seriously hurt, maybe even died from such a high fall. I suppose we could lock her in a room or tie her up when she's outside." Rob was thinking out loud and instantly knew from Kristine's reaction to his idea that she wouldn't buy those solutions.

"Rob, if she was in an asylum that's what they'd do, you know that. No, I won't make our home a prison for her, and I know you really wouldn't want that either."

All the bread was eaten; the coffee pot emptied and still no real solution for Sophie's unpredictable antics could be agreed upon, but they did both agree on one thing, tamperproof locks had to be installed on all windows and doors that Sophie could reach.

The Past Still Haunts The Future

Kristine had come from the same Sweden that her in-laws Marten and Hanna had left behind, but she and Marten had come for very different purposes. Kristine's Sweden had been hard, but not cruel as it had been to Marten. Still, Kristine's Sweden in the late 1890s held little hope for an ambitious young women who wished for independence and upward social mobility.

After Kristine's mother died, her brothers returned to their farms and her older sisters went back to their live-in positions at a nearby manor house. Emma, just a child, went to live with one of her sisters. Kristine, who was known as Kersti when she lived in Sweden, moved with her father to the city of Malmo. During those years the young woman found employ as a *piga* or maid in the rooming houses and inns that huddled around the harbor of the bustling port city. The work was physically hard and humiliating, but even as she labored at her position's demeaning tasks, the belief there was more to life than emptying some sailor's chamber pot or warding off drunken traveler's advances burned like a nighttime ember within her. For Kersti, those years only strengthened her desire to find a way to escape to a better life. Daily, she heard tales told by travelers returning from America and other distant lands. There in those far-off lands of mystery, opportunities abound, fortunes could be made, and possibilities beyond one's imagination awaited anyone willing to risk all and go, even a young woman. The young dreamer quickly became infected with *America Fever*. She was equally convinced that a destiny among America's wealthy households could be hers, if only she, alone or with others, stepped onto that gangplank, boarded the steamer and left all that she knew behind. She never believed that America's streets were actually lined with gold, but she did know that a different life awaited her, hopefully filled with adventure, excitement and opportunity.

It had not been so for Marten and Hanna, they had come to escape poverty and want. Though they had not originally come from homes and lives of poverty, the cruel hand of fate found Marten, Hanna, and a young daughter living out their days on a poor farm for the destitute. The economic conditions of rural Sweden during the 1800s had robbed so many of their modest lives and taken away their hope of reversing those conditions.

Fueled by Sweden's agricultural and economic conditions during the 1800s, several movements arose that gave a glimmer of hope to many Swedes, especially those in rural regions where agricultural adversity created the most hardship. The first vision of a new and better life was offered by the persistent visits of steamship line agents who hawked the American Dream as a cheap ticket aboard transatlantic steamers, often in conditions that cattle would find objectionable. The second glimmer of hope, often more substantial and immediate, was a religious movement of a personal spiritual awakening that rippled through the impoverished regions of the old country and challenged its believers to a deeper level of faith. With nothing to lose, Marten, his wife, and their young daughter boarded a steamer for the New World. Several days after the couple arrived in New York, Hanna gave birth to their first American child, a son they named Robert.

Marten was invigorated. His newly found yet evolving passions dominated his American life. First he vowed to work for no one except himself and God, and at the same time to spread the word of his religious enlightenment. To accomplish this he saw his immigrating countrymen as a resource; as these travelers entered this new experience called America, Marten understood what they needed and wanted. He vowed to help both himself and the immigrants. In Sweden, Marten had fallen to such unimaginable lows that he now was willing to gamble all to make his new life successful, and that is exactly what he did. First he drove a team delivering lumber, and then he became a foreman for that same business. But Marten was thirsty, and soon he began selling the lumber directly to builders until he decided that he too could build and sell houses.

Marten had a savvy sense about business and people. Directed by the tenets of his deepening religious convictions, he quickly gained the trust of those who looked to him for help and used every morsel of his evolving world to grow his business. Soon almost every new home was a Marten Johansson and Sons home, in whole or part. Business propelled Marten onward, but his faith guided his passionate work at the immigrant missions. Still, it was not enough for an ambitious man. Soon his calling at the piers became invitations to gather and worship in his home. These gatherings and families became the foundation for a small church of likeminded believers. Marten had demanded much of himself and now he demanded much of his growing family.

Challenges of Food and Faith

"Mama, does Sophie have to make such a mess when she eats? I'm losing my appetite, really I am." This time it was William's inquiring voice, but everyone felt the strain of Sophie's eating habits.

Kristine didn't answer immediately. She lifted the spoon of mashed-up food to Sophie's mouth but the girl refused to open for it. Kristine, whose own evening meal still remained untouched, sighed with exasperation. She tried enticing the child with the spoonful of soft food once more. No luck here, so she resorted to the only sure way of getting Sophie to eat, a small dollop of food onto her plate. The child scooped at it with her fingers then inserted the mush into her mouth—or rather, across her mouth and face.

"I know it's difficult to watch her eat," Kristine began. "But she needs to watch the family eat, that's how she learns. She's so good at copying others and if she sees us sit together and eat, maybe she'll learn how to use the spoon rather than just using her fingers and hands."

Willi spoke up, "Mama, she uses her hands now. Maybe if you put her hand on the spoon, then put your hand over hers and we all do the same, she'll understand."

"Let's try it," Mama said.

Sophie was delighted with all the attention and promptly complied with holding the spoon and letting Kristine guide her hand. One spoonful in then a second one, then a third was begun, but Sophie had a mind of her own. Whoosh! Instantly the contents of the newly filled spoon flew through the air and landed squarely in the center of the table, splattering onto Poppa and William's plates.

"Enough!" Poppa said, rising abruptly from the table. "Enough experimenting. My dinner is over. I'll be in the parlor."

Try as she might, Sophie could not learn to use eating utensils. Her limbs, especially her hands, didn't seem to cooperate. Even the simple spoon seemed impossible to master, even after Kristine bent one to fit comfortably into her hand. It seemed as if nature's way would be the only way that she could learn to feed herself, at least for now. So Mama began to make new foods for Sophie, ones that she could eat with her hands and not create such a mess. Slowly, meal by meal, the family and Sophie learned to tolerate each other and soon mealtimes became more about eating than arguing.

But life is that wind that blows both foul and fair and the family so wished that all challenges were as resolvable as the dinner table messes.

* * * * * * * *

Sophie had to be watched carefully all the time now and that meant on the Lord's Day too. Rob had become the Sunday school superintendent of Marten's small but growing church. The mantle of church leadership fell first to his oldest son, then in time it would be shared by others. So it came as an expectation that Rob would not only teach, but also host the many meetings and classes of the fledging congregation that had found stability and nourishment in Marten's mission work with the immigrants at the piers.

The littlest children attended a nursery program and the older children Sunday school. The parents were expected at worship service, but little Sophie just couldn't adjust to that rigor. No, she'd cry or scream or make noise and no matter if Willi or Beth tried to take her with them, it just didn't work. Everyone became annoyed and paid more attention to her than the minister, which in turn caused quite a stir in the congregation. There was only one answer.

"Rob," Kristine began one Sunday after dinner. "We can't continue taking Sophie to the church on Sundays. I've had enough of all those old women cackling behind my back."

"I know Kristine, I'm just not sure what to do."

"Well, I'm just going to stay home with her, that's what I'm going to do," Kristine exclaimed.

"I don't like that idea, the whole family has to go to service together. Father has made it clear that we must set the example. It's unacceptable to him if we don't all go, but..." he hesitated for what seemed like an eternity, "... maybe Sophie would get better if we didn't take her where there are so many people. At least for a while."

Kristine kept quiet. She knew when to let Rob think.

"We can't have another day like today," Rob reluctantly admitted.

So the plan was made, but they both knew that Marten would not approve of their decision. Kristine would stay home with the child, which maybe would fit her better than going to church every Sunday anyway. She was an Old World Lutheran and in Sweden the Church was not so involved in one's daily affairs. One went most Sundays if possible, but certainly on special occasions and holidays. But Kristine had not married into a traditional Lutheran family, for here among Rob's family the fervor of religion was a way of life and it drove everything.

It wasn't that Kristine didn't have faith or beliefs; it's just that hers were different. She had made this choice, to marry Rob, to join this family and she did it willingly, but deep within her that flame of her independence still flickered. After she and Rob made the decision about Sophie and church, Kristine joined the spiritual worship only when it occurred in their home, which was often, but she seldom appeared at the little church down the street. The church and its activities became less and less important until finally the minister paid Kristine a visit, the first of many.

"He just doesn't understand, Rob. He comes into our house, he enjoys my cooking and drinks my special fruit juice and then gives me one of his *talks*. If he's bringing me the Lord's message, then the Lord doesn't understand, either. Sophie is God's child as much as any member of our family. Honestly, I don't appreciate his stern talks about how my not attending church is paving the path to eternity's halls of fire. The Swedes are going to be so surprised when they get to Heaven and find someone else there besides themselves." Rob knew better than to challenge Kristine on this subject, he had enough challenges with Marten over the entire affair.

For Kristine there was a bit of sweetness to their decision. It allowed her to shine with a special Sunday dinner for the family. She used her fine china and pressed the linens. The plates were carefully warmed, and she made Rob's favorite foods. If the day happened to coincide with someone's birthday, dessert for the day was their favorite pie, or, if they preferred, a fluffy chiffon cake. Sunday was also a day for visiting, so after the Sunday dinner was eaten and enjoyed, friends and relatives would often gathered in the Johnson's parlor to enjoy more of Kristine's culinary creations, drink endless cups of coffee, and engage in conversation that now was mostly about the conflict in Europe and how America was becoming involved.

" …and then Sven Pederson told me about how they called up his son and he leaves next week for training. So far William is still too young to be called up, but so many in the congregation might have family that will have to go." Rob had spent much of his breakfast time telling Kristine about yesterday's conversations and what was in the newspaper that lately he seemed to read in its entirety.

"Kristine, there is something else that worries me. The paper had this article about how doctors are being asked to report all their cases of epilepsy and certain other mental illnesses to the state. There is renewed talk of programs of institutionalism. The authorities worry that the feeble-minded will become criminals and cause a rise in crime." He paused as if reluctant to go on. "Perhaps it's because of the military call up, but the authorities also fear that the women will become easy prey for men and that they will spread disease and bare children out of wedlock who will carry their feeblemindedness with them. Even though Sophie is still a child and not yet old enough to bare a child, I worry that the authorities will consider Sophie part of this group and identify her."

Kristine said nothing but kneaded the bread she was making with an intensified vigor. Making bread relieved her stress, and these days she made a lot of bread.

"Rob, now that Sophie is growing up she often acts quickly and independently. She resents being watched so closely. I worry that someday she'll slip away and no one will see her go. The children aren't always here to give an extra set of eyes and Dottie is just beginning to get into things, too. Sophie seems so curious about everything and just wants to go find the next thing that attracts her attention. I think she'd just follow her shadow down the street if she could."

There, she'd said it, actually voiced the concern she'd had for so long. There really weren't many solutions and any plausible ones, like more locks, cost money. The war was beginning to take its toll on everyone and spending even a little extra money now was a concern, even if it was for a very good cause.

Rob didn't react, he just sat there drinking his coffee and reading his paper. *Had he even heard me?* She wondered.

"Kristine, for now, just try to be more watchful," he finally said as he picked up his coat to go to the office. "I'll see if there are some more old locks hanging around the warehouse that I could use. There isn't much work right now with the war and all, people don't want to build new houses and we need to watch every penny we spend. Maybe the girls or Hanna can help you more. Willi spends too much time playing games with her friends, she's the one who could watch Sophie a bit closer." Conversation over. He opened the door and left for the office.

Not what I wanted to hear. Secretly Kristine had hoped that maybe they could hire someone other than family to come in and help for a couple hours each week, but that was hoping for too much.

That summer proved more trying than usual. Of course there was the wave of stifling heat but there was much more. Rob gave Kristine less and less money for groceries, and the news from the foreign war hit home time and time again. Boys from the neighborhood perished, the families wept in silence and aloud and even the little congregation was not spared. Everyone was called on to do more with less. Even Sophie could feel the tension and pushed her limits to the extreme.

A Welcome Surprise

"Hot," she said aloud to the empty kitchen. A smile crept upward as Kristine blew a cooling breath across the cup's steaming contents. She now had an excuse to relax and slowly sip her morning coffee. Such serendipitous moments gave her precious personal time, something that was a rare commodity these days.

Sophie was growing, developing in many ways and very active. It was normal for children to explore, but Sophie could no longer be trusted to stay where she was put. Kristine also knew that of all her children, Willi was Sophie's best guardian.

Kristine began to sip the cooling coffee. The fresh breeze from the open window felt so good that it was easy to sit and linger just a moment or two more, to let her thoughts wander into places she rarely allowed herself to explore. The selfish thoughts and the coffee, this morning both were good.

All our children are such individuals.

William has a good mind, especially with all these new mechanical inventions. I don't understand them, but he does and that will be his future. He's adventurous but sometimes that boy likes the easiest way best. I do worry about him, though. Recently he seems to be pushing back against so many things. His friends are changing, too. They used to be from our family or from the church, but now they're from the wider neighborhood. I can feel him being drawn to their world, one very different from Rob's world. I've seen that world and I know there are real risks for a young man.

She sipped more coffee.

Beth is my right hand, to be sure. She's so trustworthy and capable, such a hardworking girl. She always tries to make things work out for the best. I couldn't make our home function without Beth, but I know that I'm also hard on her. I don't mean to be, but old thoughts and biting words just jump forward to my tongue. I wish I could forget those cruel words that followed my every move when I began to work. Those years in Malmo were difficult and trying. I was so young and so much was expected of me. I tried so hard, just like Beth, but in the eyes of my overseer I always fell short. I've tried to forget the harsh, stinging words that assailed my every move, to find better things to say, but the old words and criticisms worm their way forward from the back of my mind. I cannot stop their creep forward, especially when Beth tries so hard to do the same things I struggled with years ago.

Another sip of coffee while Kristine gazed pensively at the landscape beyond her kitchen window, but the landscape she saw in her mind was hundreds of miles away in time almost forgotten by most.

Now, Willi's different from all the others. That girl has a mind of her own and knows just where she's going in life. It's just that it's usually in the opposite direction than everyone else is going, but her heart, it's huge. She tries everyone's patience, but at the end of the day, you just have to smile and let her be herself.

Kristine caught herself smiling at the thought of Willi's antics and finished the last of her now cooled coffee.

Of course Dottie is just a baby, but already I notice she has a personality. I doubt if the child will ever have a mean bone in her body.

As the day wore on, Kristine found herself thinking more and more about the children.

Little Sophie has a personality too and she lets everyone know just what she wants, likes or doesn't like. But it is her singing voice that was just a bit of a miracle. For sure the little child has words and uses them, sometimes very effectively, but her words are her own. It is as if she has invented her own language and everyone has to learn her ways, but she doesn't ever learn ours. But where, Mama wondered, did that singing voice of hers come from? What a miracle.

Kristine remembered that day of discovery with a warm, amazed feeling. Beth had come running into the kitchen and in an excited voice exclaimed, "Mama come quickly, you've got to hear what Sophie can do!" then ran back into the parlor.

The children had been listening to the new Victrola phonograph. Rob, who rarely spent extra money, had surprised the family with this extraordinary gift. Then he put William in charge of the machine, with some rules of course, so that he could settle back and simply watch his family enjoy the gift.

William was the only other person Rob wanted putting records on the phonograph's turntable. He taught William how to crank the mainspring to adjust the right tension and when to release the brake lever that set the record spinning. Ever so carefully, he placed the needle upon the spinning disc. The sound was magical and mysterious. How did the voices get inside that record, and more importantly, how could the phonograph bring the music to their ears? Most of the family's recordings were hymns and operatic selections, but several new recordings were the children's favorites. These wartime records of rousing patriotic music were the songs that fascinated Sophie and she listened to them over and over again.

Beth continued telling Mama what had happened. "After your favorite song was finished, William put on the marching music." Kristine loved to listen to the rich grand voice of Enrico Caruso. As his voice filled the parlor she was drawn backward in time to an evening long ago. Kristine's influential employer had invited her young lady's maid to join the family and adoring patrons for the evening's entertainment, a private concert by the world-renowned tenor. Though her seat was in the rear of the parlor, she listened in rapt silence to the majesty of Caruso's music. To hear him again was one of her truest pleasures. Secretly she believed Rob had bought the machine mostly for her—a way to say he cared about her and appreciated all she did for the family—as the first and only records he purchased originally were her favorites. Words of affection from Rob were few; it was his actions that counted. That was just his way.

Beth continued, "We all told him to play the tunes again. When William lifted the needle we couldn't believe what we heard. Listen, William's going to play the record again."

Martial music filled the room, then without warning William lifted the needle arm from the record. A lilting voice filled the room and there with perfect pitch and voiced lyrics, Sophie sang the words of the Great War that raged in Europe:

"Over there, over there,
Send the word, send the word over there
That the Yanks are coming, the Yanks are coming
The drums are rum-tumming everywhere"

Song after song, either by herself or singing along with the great artists of the day, the Johnson's home was filled with stirring music and soon all the younger children were marching about with broomstick firearms, singing "It's a long way to Tipperary, it's a long way back home" and tenting under blanket-covered kitchen chairs.

Kristine smiled. *Yes, my children are truly special, all of them.*

Winds of War

"It wasn't good, Rob," his father began. "This morning I had to fire that new man we hired last month, the tall lanky German, Hans. I caught him stealing and we had words and he threatened all of us, you and your family too."

Marten's business had been good for his family. The boys all had respectable jobs at the lumberyard and even in these tough times there was a paycheck, albeit meager, for each family. Marten Johansson and Sons was the best lumberyard around, so if they were having a hard time, everyone else was feeling the pinch too.

Kristine kept peeling potatoes but her mind was on the conversation. She worried a lot now, there was so little money, the children were growing, Sophie was so much worse and there were so many needs to fill.

"I think Hans is harmless, but be extra careful tonight, Rob. He kept talking about the war, about how powerful Germany was and how they would have their way in the end. It sounded like gibberish, half German and half broken English, but I had no trouble understanding those angry words."

Marten pushed his chair back and stood up to leave. "Kristine, I heard a story today. Is it true that Sophie ran away again?"

Taken aback by the question, Kristine wheeled around and stared squarely at Marten. "What did you hear? Who did you hear it from? Tell me, I need to know."

There had been an incident today and she'd hoped to keep it a secret from Rob and the others, but now, everyone was staring at Kristine and waiting for Marten's answer.

Marten looked about, realizing Rob knew nothing about today and answered carefully.

"My delivery driver Swenson told me. Said he saw Beth and Willi walking Sophie up the hill from Center Street. He stopped and asked if he could help since Sophie didn't seem to want to go with them, but they said "Thanks, but no thanks." He watched them until they got here to Hunt Street, just in case they had more trouble, but they were almost home and so he left. Sophie was really having a tough time."

"The girls were doing an errand for me, Marten," Kristine answered. "Willi wanted to take Sophie with them but she got tired and wanted to go home before the errand was finished." Kristine's answer was partially true, but not completely, and she hoped her lie wouldn't be noticed. Marten seemed satisfied and left.

She may have fooled Marten but not Rob.

"Kristine, you better tell me what happened today." Rob was adamant.

"Sophie was playing outside on the lawn one minute and then she was gone," Kristine began. "We thought she was playing that new hiding game she made up, but after a few minutes the children knew she wasn't here."

Rob paced up and down in front of the table as he listened to Kristine.

"We searched everywhere, but Sophie was gone. I was frantic with worry and as the children and I were planning an all out neighborhood search, there was a knock on the door. It was the delivery boy from the Center Street Grocery who told us to go down and get Sophie. She had gone to the grocery's ice cream counter all on her own and was sitting there eating ice cream and waiting for us. But of course, she liked it there and didn't want to come back home, so Willi and Beth went down to fetch her. Of course I gave the girls money to pay for the ice cream, but the shop keeper wouldn't take it."

Rob stopped pacing, looked out the window and just stared. "Kristine, I'll be in my office. I need to work on that new job I just got. Call me when supper is ready."

The Spark

So much seemed to be happening that summer. A heat wave continued for days. The heat kept the children from playing at the glass pile, and far off across the back lot, Tiffany's factory workers hung from the windows for some small relief. The city decided to open one of the water barrels nearby and let it run in the street, much to the delight of all the neighborhood children. The relief was only temporary.

It had been weeks since Sophie ran away, but once again Poppa couldn't sleep. Maybe it was the heat, his worry about Sophie, or even his father's lingering warning about Hans. He slipped out of bed and pulled on his work pants and slippers. Kristine stirred.

"Where are you going, Rob?"

"Don't know if the back door is locked, just checking."

"You checked it an hour ago."

"Once more won't hurt."

It was a dark night with almost no wind. From the back door he could see the dim glow from deep within the Tiffany Furnace and tonight, even the silhouetted shadowy figures of men working late into the night were clearly visible. He closed the door and walked down the hallway to the front entrance.

Rob opened the front door, walked out onto the porch and looked down the street towards the gates of the lumberyard's closest entrance. It was a big yard with piles of lumber stored at least twice the height of a man; a shop for turning custom moldings; and a huge warehouse that stored windows, doors, paint, shingles and even exotic woods from all over the world. The business was originally sited along the bank of a backwater bay. It had been easy for the barges to deliver lumber and goods, but then the railroad lines were laid and the business grew outward on land it claimed from nature. One by one the houses came until the neighborhood huddled closely around the rapidly expanding contractor's business. The neighborhood, built in whole or part with products from Marten Johansson and Sons, climbed the gentle hills that rose upward from the bay. At first the houses distanced themselves from each other, but with time, other buildings rose wherever space allowed building until the neighborhood was congested and crowded.

Rob and Kristine's house was almost at the top of the Hunt Street hill. Even though it was several blocks away, Rob could see much of the lumberyard from his porch. It was his father's business and thankfully, as jobs were scarce, most of his family still worked for Marten. Privately, Rob and his brothers were a bit worried since Marten had recently taken on a partner, his recently widowed son-in-law. Amongst the brothers there had been some resentment about their father's decision, but Rob reasoned that Marten was more worried about his grandchildren's futures than the elevation of the outsider over his sons. Perhaps Marten wanted his son-in-law safely employed in a manner that tied him to the family unit and employed in a position Marten controlled.

Marten did like control and sometimes that control—especially in his sons' lives—was too much. Rob hoped his father knew what he was doing. He was the company's only architect and designed most of the houses his father built, but the young architect wanted to do more than just work for his father, he wanted his own business. The young man had dreams, dreams that he hoped could evolve beyond his father's control.

Though it was some distance away, Rob's eyes caught what seemed like a tiny glow within the lumberyard's clutter. Why would anyone be carrying a lantern in the lumberyard at this time of the night? Something was wrong, but before Rob's brain made sense of the light, he smelled the smoke.

There is a fatal moment of confusion when reality and desperation collide. He tried to reason the moment away but it was not possible. His brain was screaming an alarm, but his voice failed him and his legs refused to move.

"Fire! The lumberyard's on fire!"

What to do? Pull the firebox alarm, yes, pull the alarm. Where is it? Think. Rob, think! Up the hill, by the trolley stop.

He felt his feet pounding on the cobblestone street. *Don't trip on the tracks. There's the box, break the glass, pull the lever.* He looked down the street; his house and family were now between him and the fire. *The family, the houses are too close. Get the family out, now!* Far away he could hear the clanging of a bell, the fire bell. He knew the alarm was sounding.

Kristine met Rob on the porch. "Willi and Beth are already getting Sophie and Dottie ready to leave the house and William is on his way to the lumberyard office. He has your keys to open the gate for the firemen. Oh Rob, this is terrible, just terrible. I'll be okay, just put your boots on before you go down there. Marten is on his way down the hill to the yard. I'll take the children to your parent's house, it's further away from the fire." Kristine handed Rob his boots and the young man suddenly realized he was now barefoot, his slippers somewhere on the hillside road.

Gripping Sophie's wrist tightly, Willi pulled her struggling sister up the hillside towards their grandparent's house. The child pulled against her sister's grip, wincing in pain, but Willi kept the tight grip knowing that at all costs Sophie must not break loose. Beth, only steps behind, clutched a swaddled baby Dottie firmly in her arms. Once the girls reached Marten's house, the full fury of the fire became visible through the large double window in their grandparent's parlor.

"I'm scared, Willi!" Beth's voice broke. "I can't stop shaking, I don't think the firemen can put it out, the fire's too big." Beth wasn't easily scared and if she was scared, Willi thought she should be also. Fear seemed everywhere; there was no escaping its crawling fingers.

"Beth, don't you think it's getting awfully hot in here? I don't mean warm, I mean hot, really hot. Can this room explode into flames?" Panic was beginning to seize Willi too.

"Get back from the windows, Willi. It's the glass, it's getting hot from the heat of the fire." Beth reached out to touch the glass but quickly withdrew her fingers. She felt the wall and windowsill. "The wall and windows are getting hot too. Maybe we should leave?"

"Mama told us to stay here Beth, where would we go?"

"Mama," Beth called out. "Where are you? Are we safe here? Mama? Mama! Where are you?"

Mama didn't answer. Beth began to search the hallway and kitchen for whoever remained and found a fearful *farmor*, her grandmother Hanna stuffing a satchel with whatever was close at hand. She looked at Beth, answering her questions with fear-filled eyes and rapid Swedish.

"Beth, what did she say?"

"I think she said that Mama went to our house to help Poppa and we need to stay right here."

The fire raged on but the children could no longer stand near the windows. Dottie cried and Beth's arms ached from holding and rocking her. Sophie had long ago begun a low whimpering cry that would not stop and retreated into the shadows of the room's farthest corner. She tucked her head between her arms and curled into a ball, stiff and resistant to each of Willi's touches.

"Well, at least she's not trying to run away," Willi reasoned and just let her be.

"Oh dear God, what was that?" Beth exclaimed.

A deafening roar rose from the belly of the fire and an explosion of burning debris rose high into the night sky, hesitated for a moment, then cascaded as a burning shower on its fall back to earth.

The girls looked on in horror as they watched the entire warehouse collapse into itself.

* * * * * * * *

Sunlight was just beginning to lighten the sky but Marten and Hanna's kitchen had already become the gathering place for family. One by one, each unkempt and smoke-laden family member entered the kitchen and took a cup of coffee from the enormous pot that seemed to be ever present on Hanna's kitchen range. Kristine had brought bread and spreads from her kitchen, but no one seemed to have an appetite.

"Marten, the fire captain's at the front door," a voice from the hallway announced.

"Come in, Captain. Come have a cup of coffee," Marten said.

The fireman entered, willingly accepting the hot mug from Hanna. "Sit down, Captain. Tell us the latest."

"It's bad, Marten," he began. "We were only able to save the business office and that's because it wasn't attached to the rest of the buildings. Only a couple of homes close to the yard had damage, mostly burned roofs or siding. Luckily the offshore winds blew much of the fire out over the bay. Because of that, we were able to keep the fire from spreading. Had that not been, the whole neighborhood would have burned."

The Fire Captain paused and composed himself before continuing. "However, I do have some tragic news. One of our firemen, O'Conner, didn't make it. We found his body this morning... a wall fell on him when the warehouse collapsed. He left a wife and three children. He was a good man and one damn good firefighter."

Kristine let out a deep gasp. "Oh my Lord, oh my Lord!"

"One more thing Marten, we think the fire was set. Had all the hallmarks of arson. The police will be there most of the day, so you'll need to stay off the site that is until they're finished with their investigation. They'll be up to see you later just to let you know their preliminary findings."

The fire captain excused himself and quietly let himself out of the house. The stunned family just sat, fixed in place by the morning's shocking news. Mama cried softly but no one spoke. Only shock and fear crept onto their faces. Each in his or her own way knew that life had changed dramatically; what their life had been just yesterday could never be again. There would be much to deal with tomorrow and the day after that and for many days beyond. What they could not see on that emotionally charged morning was how life could now move forward. No, that unknown could not even be imagined by anyone.

Changes

The winds of change had blown briskly. After the fire, life assumed a different tempo. At first the shock of the disaster and especially the death of the fireman cast a shadow of darkness over every undertaking. Change was measured first in days, then months, and finally in years. The lumberyard was reestablished and some modest home construction resumed. As time went on, Marten began to withdraw from the daily grind of business, delegating the decision-making more frequently to others. The trauma of the fire had been hardest on him, but he had tenaciously stayed at its helm. Now however, the business was beginning to suffer as Marten's health deteriorated.

Kristine had just put freshly made bread into the oven when a sharp rap on the kitchen door startled her.

"Marten?"

"Kristine, is Rob home? I need to talk with him and could we talk privately in the parlor? I've asked the rest of the boys to come over too. I hope you don't mind, it's important."

The words caught Kristine by total surprise. She hardly expected Marten to appear at her back door midway through the workday and she was even more surprised to see him dressed in his finest suit and not his work clothes. She quickly studied the aging man and did not like what she saw.

"Of course Marten, come in. I'll get Rob."

Kristine didn't even bother to knock on the young architect's office door, instead she just quickly let herself into the office.

"Rob, something's wrong. Marten is here, your brothers are coming and Marten wants everyone to meet in our parlor. What on earth could be in the wind? He looks so pale."

Once assembled, the impromptu family business meeting dragged on into the afternoon. Marten's business partner was summoned and finally the attorney for Marten Johansson and Sons appeared at the front door. The air was filled with shouts and strident voices. Words like lawsuits, damages, negligence, responsibility, and retirement were yelled so loudly that they could be heard right though the closed doors. Rob called for refills of coffee and more plates of meat and cheese. Finally all parties involved were satisfied with the arrangements. The sun was low in the evening sky as the last legal document was signed and notarized. The difficult and trying day was finally over.

Rob saw the final family member out through the front door and returned to the kitchen carrying one remaining plate of meat and cheese. Kristine poured each of them one last half cup of coffee and Rob quietly sat at the table and picked at the leftovers.

"What happened, Rob?"

Marten's eldest son was silent for a few more long moments then raised his eyes and began to tell Kristine the details of the afternoon.

"Well, to start with, Marten is being forced to retire from the business. That is probably good, as his health is suffering. That's something we've all seen for some time now. The lumberyard and the home building unit will be run exclusively by Marten's partner Rawson, but in the short term Marten will advise him as necessary. In the longer view, Marten has narrowly escaped some very serious charges that could have resulted in lawsuits that he probably would have lost. Either way, it would have been very expensive. It will still be difficult, but the rest of us will keep our jobs, at least for the time being, but we'll have to think about the future as the home building unit may be sold and that's the unit that gives me a job."

Eventually Marten and Hanna sold their home in the city and moved to a small farm in the country. This new venue afforded the couple a community of like-minded countrymen in a fresh and clean environment. From his new home, Marten could remain active in both of his life's passions: religious mission work among his countrymen, and his role as an absentee advisor to the running of his old business.

Consequences

Without Marten and Hanna, there were fewer relatives nearby to help Rob and Kristine with the demands of their growing family. Kristine worried that without Marten's daily involvement in the business, Rob wouldn't have time for his family. She was right, work did take more time and he spent much less time with her and the children, but what she hadn't planned on was that Rob was changing, too. The demands of work chaffed at him. He was easily irritated and grew less tolerant of problems that arose with the children, especially William.

All the children had escaped to play, but today Beth lingered until the others were out of sight. "Mama," she began. "I need to talk to you."

"Of course Beth, what's on your mind?"

"I don't know if I should say anything, but did you know that William didn't go to school today?"

"What? What are you saying, Beth?"

Beth swallowed hard then began. "Mama, I don't want to tell tales, but this isn't the first time. William goes into the school building with us, then rather than go to his class he goes to the boy's lavatory. This time I watched and when he came out, he looked around and walked out of the school building. He didn't show up again until school was dismissed."

Kristine was visibly shaken by her daughter's news, but it wasn't exactly a surprise. She had worried about William for some time now. She just couldn't put her finger on the problem, but each day that uncomforting feeling of knowing something isn't quite right persisted. Mothers have a way of sensing those things.

"Thank you Beth. I'll take care of this. Don't bother your Poppa with what you told me. I'll talk to William. Now run off and enjoy what's left of the afternoon."

Kristine didn't know what she was going to do. When it came to the family, Rob was in charge. He used the Bible as his handbook and disciplined accordingly. Usually it was fair and compassionate, but lately he was so irritated. The new management at the lumberyard had cut down on the time he could work on his building designs and instead had put him in the cabinet shop to fill orders. He possessed strong carpentry skills, but it wasn't his passion. The manual work tired him so when he came home each evening, he'd simply eat supper then retire. If he wanted to work on his drawings and plans, he had to do it before he went to work in the morning, so while it was still dark, one would find Rob drawing in his office. It was taking a toll on everyone.

"You're not going to tell Poppa are you?" William pleaded with his mother.

"No, not this time, William. Also, you're not going to do anything to your sister for telling me about what she observed," Kristine added. William's anger with his sister had been so evident when Mama confronted her son about his day's escapades that she momentarily worried about Beth.

"Where did you go? What where you thinking?"

It was do or die for William and he knew that he needed Mama on his side. "Well, I know how hard it is for you and Poppa now and how there isn't any extra money for anything. So, I found someone who would hire me to do some work for them. I had hoped that I could earn a little money so I could do some things that I wanted to do." Then he quickly added, "And maybe give you some more money for the house. The problem was it was during school hours, so I went to work a few days each week."

Kristine sat still, her mouth agape.

"Mama, I want to leave school and go to work full time. I'm not good at school and I hate being in those boring classes. If I could find a job I could learn new skills, make money and take care of myself."

The boy had come this far so now he had nothing to lose at telling Mama more.

"I know how important Sunday school and regular school are to Poppa, but honestly, they aren't important to me. I want to do other things, maybe even sign onto a ship and travel to another country, but I don't want to do the things that Poppa and you want me to do."

Kristine could feel something inside her awakening long stilled thoughts and dreams. She had hardly been William's age when she told her father that she no longer wanted to stay in Sweden, that she wanted to go to America and make a different life for herself. She also knew that William was more like her in temperament then his father. She might talk some sense into him today, but someday soon he would leave and neither she nor Rob would be able to stop him. At least he had not said he wanted to be a soldier and go to war.

"William, there is much you've just told me. For right now I'm going to ask you to return to school, to do as you're instructed by your father and by me. When the time is right, I promise you I will talk to Poppa. Meanwhile, talk to the man who hired you and see if you can work after school or on Saturday. Maybe for now that is a solution, but be careful. I know that sometimes people who hire young lads like you, will ask them to do things that are unlawful or just on the edge of the law. You'll meet other lads who may not know right from wrong and you must, I mean must, keep the authorities from thinking something is wrong within our family. Promise me, you'll think carefully about your actions. Promise!"

"I promise, Mama, I promise."

William's Broken Promise

"Mama, Mama!" Beth ran into the kitchen exclaiming breathlessly, "Come quickly, Mama, there are two policemen at the front door and they have William with them."

Kristine dropped what she was doing and ran down the hallway to answer the door. "Beth," she said, "Go get Poppa, right now."

"Is this the Johnson household?" the first officer inquired.

"Yes it is, and why do you have our son with you?"

William stood between the two burly uniformed officers, his head bowed and his gaze fixed exclusively on the porch floorboards. Kristine's heart sank as she realized that the boy was handcuffed to one of the officers.

"Mrs. Johnson, we need to speak with you and your husband about your son. We can do it here on the porch or inside." the officer continued.

"Oh, come inside, that would be best."

Kristine could hear Rob coming in from the office, his footsteps pounding and deliberate. She knew even before he opened the parlor doors that his anger was intense.

"What is going on?" He thundered.

"Mr. Johnson, my name is officer O'Mallory and this is officer Kessel. Your son was caught stealing from one of the pushcart peddlers near the town square. He's never been in trouble with the police before, so we brought him home rather than take him to the station."

By now, both Kristine and Rob were pale and limp with shock. The children, scared by the presence of the police with William in their custody, hid their sister in the kitchen.

"Willi, keep Sophie very close to you, don't let her get away and run into the parlor. This is bad and we don't want to make it worse," Beth instructed her sister.

Rob, not a tall or muscular man, pulled himself up squarely in front of the officer but his gaze was fixed totally on William. "Officer, tell me what happened, everything that happened and William, look at me!" Rob was so angry it was hard for him to sound in control and somewhat civil.

Officer O'Mallory began, "For a while we've been watching a gang of neighborhood hooligans. They've been giving the storekeepers and peddlers trouble. They would do what we call a *bait and steal* scheme, that is they would create a reason for the shopkeeper or peddler to be distracted, then the boys would rush in and steal things, mostly food, while the peddler wasn't watching his goods. Originally, these thefts were little more than a nuisance for the merchants and didn't really do them much harm. Little by little, the thefts added up and now it's become a problem. Money is so tight now because of the war, even little thefts hurt the peddlers."

William squirmed in place, extremely uncomfortable as the story played out.

"The peddler assaulted today was an old man whose only livelihood is selling his fruit and vegetables. The boys began their scheme but this time your boy was a part of the gang. Someone told us they heard one of the leaders calling out '*Hey Swede Boy, it's your turn. Show us your stuff. Get the fruit any way you can*'." The officer nodded towards William. "Swede Boy here pushed in and grabbed the fruit, handfuls of it. The peddler tried to stop him. Someone shoved the peddler, maybe your boy, maybe someone else, but he fell to the street and then his heavy cart—complete with all his fruit—collapsed, right on top of the old man."

Kristine couldn't contain herself, "Was he hurt? Was he killed?"

"He wasn't killed, but he was seriously hurt." Kessel said. "He's at Doc Rabb's office now."

O'Mallory continued, "All the peddler's produce was ruined and his cart will need extensive repair. The other boys escaped to the their hovels near the meadows, that we know, but we caught your boy. At first I thought we should just take him to the station, really teach him a lesson, but when we learned that William was Marten Johansson's grandson, Kessel here suggested a different path of action."

"I once worked with Johansson," Kessel began, "to end some problems we had with some new immigrant families. That's how I learned that the lumber merchant had a solid reputation for helping immigrants when they first arrive in this country. Marten was there on the piers when his countrymen and others came off the ships and helped them get started in this country by finding them housing and jobs-families that settled right here in our community. In this neighborhood we're all immigrants from somewhere. He even helped some of my relatives though we weren't Swedes. Your boy was new to the gang and since it's his first problem with the law, I thought it might be time to return Johansson's kindness by not booking him and bringing him here to his family."

O'Mallory quickly added, "Don't expect you'd like that police record in the papers since rumor has it that your daughter has some mental illness and the courts have to report information like that when there's a problem. So, there will be a fine, as I've already written a report and there is the cart repair and produce to pay for, which will probably be levied against you and your wife. You'll get a summons to appear in court, but all you'll have to do is pay for the damages. I expect the boy won't be doing this again."

The officer took a key from his pocket and unlocked the handcuffs. Then they excused themselves, leaving William alone with his mother and father. William was free from the law but now under the wrath of his father.

Rob didn't say a word, not one. This man who might bluster and thunder with words, who believed that violence is not the answer, except in times of war, simply acted. Inside he quivered with rage, but his actions were slow and deliberate. He carefully unbuckled his belt, slid the thick leather from around his waist and rolled it several times around his hand. He poised, holding the belt in one hand and with the other reached out and grabbed the boy.

"Rob, don't!" Kristine pleaded. "Please don't, please!"

The words disappeared into the air, unheard. She reached out, grabbed for the belt but it was fruitless.

WHAM, WHAM, WHACK, SLAP, one lash after the other.

"Poppa, Poppa, I'll never do it again, stop, stop!" William cried out, but Rob didn't stop.

Kristine was crying, repeating her words, "Rob, stop, stop right now, please!"

The children were crying and Sophie had a convulsion, but Willi was too panicked about William to do anything for Sophie.

Then, as quickly as rage had engulfed Rob, it was gone, spent physically yes, but replaced by a catharsis of emotions that for too long had been buried and held in firm check. Torrents of tears welled up and washed across his face flowing unbridled downward onto his stiffly starched dress shirt. The shirt, like the man, withered beneath the emotional release. Rob reached out and once again grabbed his son. This time however, he pulled the boy towards him and simply held him hard and close until the son's tears matched his father's.

A Hiding Place From The Wind

Part Two: Shifting Winds

The Connecticut Countryside

Charles Chamberlain got indigestion on Monday and died on Thursday the 28th of March 1920. His family didn't think his condition serious enough to call the doctor, but when they did, it was too late. The occupants of Chamberlain's home, two sister-in laws and a boarder, moved in with kindly neighbors and relatives and the probate judge ordered that the estate be settled as soon as possible. Chamberlain's son, a businessman from New York, arrived in Connecticut within days of the farmer's death. It was an irritating interruption to the man's routine; he was a man who cared more about the business of money than his father's passing, and it took little time for him to attend to all the legal formalities of carrying out the judge's orders.

The auctioneer selected by the businessman was a local with a reputation for shrewdly milking the last penny from a farmer's worn pocket, so it would appear that the sale was a fit for all parties. However, though his occupation had allowed him to make a comfortable living, the auctioneer silently prided himself on his ability to size up a crowd and drive an auction in whatever direction he saw fit. As the years unfolded, this had become more important to the auctioneer than the commission he brought home.

"Mostly local farmers here today," the auctioneer remarked to his assistant on the morning of the auction.

"Yup, bidding isn't going to go too high, these folks aren't much better off than Chamberlain, judging from the poor repair of the farm equipment and house." The assistant was less than optimistic. "A few strangers out there though, probably relatives of the deceased," he quickly added.

"Well, let's get to it," the auctioneer said, climbing into the bed of the nearest farm wagon and rapping a metal milk can with his cane. "Morning folks, let's start with this lot of almost new milk cans."

Much to their surprise, the bidding went well for most of the morning, but by lunch time the need to eat was more pressing than the next item.

Country auctions could be festive occasions, even in March, and today the sunlight shone brightly and warmed the sheltered sides of farm buildings and walls. It was here in these warm dry warrens that the congregates to the auction uncovered their baskets of bread and cold meat, relaxed, enjoyed some neighborly conversation and perhaps a pipe of tobacco. One man however, chose a different path. The farmer whose land abutted Chamberlain's had left the auction and walked home to dine in his own kitchen, assured by Chamberlain's son that the property wouldn't be sold till much later in the day.

"How much is left to sell?" the auctioneer inquired of his clerk.

"Well, most of the big items are sold, and what's left is just what's needed to run the farm: hay, grain, and some corn seed for the spring. As far as animals, there are some chickens, two cows, a horse with some harnesses, and a wagon or two. A few more incidentals and farm tools. Really not much, why are you asking?" the clerk inquired.

"Think I'll sell it all as one lot, the land, buildings, and whatever's left. I reckon most of these locals have spent all the money they are going to spend today. Need to wrap this up."

There was one problem however—the pompous and greedy businessman son of the deceased. The auctioneer had taken an immediate dislike to the fellow and his opinion had not improved during the day. The son had taken a self-appointed position behind the auctioneer's clerk and scrutinized every name and figure that was entered into the sales book. The auctioneer wanted rid of the man, the sooner the better.

The auctioneer approached the businessman. "No need to prolong his sale now. I know you're anxious to return to the city. The best items have fetched a good price and there isn't that much left to sell. Just the run down stuff, some implements for the farm and feed for the few animals we haven't sold. I'm going to sell the rest now as one large lot, land, building and whatever hasn't sold."

"It's too early, there's more that can be sold."

"Not today, I'm finishing the sale now," the auctioneer stated.

With a few choice words, the son resumed his self-appointed post behind the clerk, but his gaze scanned the assemblage for the farmer whose land abutted Chamberlain's property. He couldn't pick him out in the crowd and that made him rather uneasy. It was important that he be here for the property sale.

The auctioneer rapped his cane on the wagon to get the crowd's attention.

"Folks, we've decided it's time to sell this farm. The clerk will now read a list of the items that are included with the sale of the house and barn."

The clerk climbed up next to the auctioneer and opened his ledger. The bidding began, but there was little interest at his starting price. He tried again, slightly lower. He sang his auction song until—finally—a bid. He tried to raise it, but nothing, just one bid.

WHAM! The auctioneer slammed his cane down on the wagon floorboards. "SOLD to the stranger in the dark suit for $2,500."

His work complete, the Yankee auctioneer climbed down from the wagon and turned deliberately to face the new owner.

"Well son, you just bought yourself a farm. Haven't seen you around these parts before. New to the area?"

"Family been here for a while," the stranger answered and nodded towards the two men with him.

"What's your name, son?"

"Johnson."

The auctioneer studied the stranger. He was balding and rather short of stature, but not old. This man in a well-cut suit certainly didn't look like any farmer he knew, but his two companions did.

"Like I say, my name's Johnson, Rob Johnson, and I'm an architect from New York. This tall fellow is my brother, Nat, and this is my father Marten. Time to come and join family."

"Well, I hope you're a praying man, Johnson," the auctioneer volunteered. "This here property will need it. Gonna need a strong back, too. The price was good, but it ain't no bargain you just bought. Ain't like those fancy N-e-e-w York properties you're used to working on. No sir, this here property will need a lot of work."

If there was one thing that the auctioneer liked more than selling, it was telling stories. He didn't need an invitation and he could tell he had a rapt audience.

"Wasn't always run down, no how. Was one of the first houses out here on the western frontier of the town, built when we were still a colony of the British crown. Choice spot too, with the water so close and protected by the hills. Best spot in the valley."

The auctioneer stopped mid-story and turned towards an argument at the clerk's desk.

"We had a bargain, Chamberlain, we shook on it. You gave your word that I'd buy the property for $2,000," the neighboring farmer yelled at the dead man's son.

"Where were you? I wasn't going to buy it for you." He retorted.

"You said it wasn't going to sell until after lunch time, you were sure of that cause there was so much that hadn't been sold yet. You said I had time to go home for dinner. You're a liar, that's what you are, probably got more money from that stranger."

It took most of the afternoon for the affairs of the auction to conclude. The buyers collected their spoils, the clerk his money, and the dead farmer's son his share. The hardscrabble farmyard emptied, the wagons rolled out, and the "tin-lizzies" grunted and groaned through the ruts and up and over the eastern hills. Only the Johnsons were left.

"Well Rob, got to do something with these animals. If you agree, I'll take them down to my barn and bring them back when you move in." Rob's brother Nat hitched the two cows behind his wagon. "Be back for the horse in about an hour. Come on Pop, you can ride down the hill with me, Rob will want to look around his new farm."

Rob welcomed the quiet. He needed to think about what was happening.

For the most part Rob was a practical calculated man, but a part of him was also a dreamer. He had found it exciting to imagine what he could become or what his life could be like if his dreams came true. It was an adventure of the mind, but now, he had taken a giant step into the unknown. When he called out his bid for the farm he moved from dreaming into doing and when the auctioneer called out the words "Sold," the winds of life burst the dream bubble and suddenly the "practical, calculated Rob" began to second-guess himself.

His father wanted him to buy this farm, and yes, he wanted to come here to be nearer to family, but what did he know about farming? Nothing, really! Sure, he could drive a team and he liked plants and gardens, but his world consisted of pens, lines, and drawing; drawings that allowed sticks of lumber to be transformed into homes that people lived in.

People needed homes here, too, his father had said. They could have the lumber shipped from the lumberyard by train and everyone would benefit. It was a plan. How could he be so excited and scared at the same time? What Rob did know, was that his family couldn't stay where they were. No, both he and Kristine knew that, it just couldn't be.

This farm would be good for the children, especially little Sophie, but life would be hard. Could they last until it got better? That he didn't know.

He had to agree with his father, it was beautiful here. The hills ringed the valley like the lip of a bowl, and here inside that bowl, the world seemed serene and quiet.

Instinctively he reached into his coat pocket withdrew his sketchbook and pen, opened to a blank page and began to do what he did best—draw. Line by line he sketched the shape of the house and barn, the curve of the abandoned road that served as a driveway up from the main North-South turnpike. He sketched the location of each window, glass eyes that radiated glows of pink and orange as the sun moved slowly towards the lip of the valley's rim. The lines of the house were classic, the lay of the land flat with the house facing the rising sun… small details, but important ones.

And there was land, lots of land, and clean air. It smelled so good, even tonight. Now all that remained was to convince Kristine that the effort and work would be worth it. The auctioneer was right, there was a lot of work to do here, much more than he realized when he bid his life's savings.

Night Shadows

Willi lay awake watching the night shadows dance across the bedroom floor. Usually on nights like this, when all the world was bathed in white moonlight and the shadows of the outside world reached their tiny part of the house, she and her sister would make a game of shadow dancing, but not tonight. Tonight the shadows scared Beth, causing her to hurry to her side of the bed and bury herself under the covers, head and all. Willi admired her sister's ability to shut out the rest of the world.

"I must stay awake," Willi voiced to the silent room. "I must listen for Poppa. I know he'll be home soon. I must stay awake."

Willi lay watching the night shadows. Beth was older and knew more about life. Maybe she too should be frightened. Willi was only eight years old, but she knew something was wrong, maybe very wrong. Now that she thought about it, there had been a lot happening these days that she didn't understand. William and Beth seemed to understand more than she did, but they wouldn't talk about it. First, there was the Western Union wire from Grandpa Marten, and Poppa left to go up to the country by himself.

Willi thought about their other visits to the country. Since Grandpa Marten had moved to Connecticut, there had been summer visits to his small farm. Willi loved those times, but visiting Grandpa Marten's farm was always a family affair. The ritual began as soon as school was out for the summer. Mama would pack an enormous basket with a picnic lunch, everyone would pack a duffle of extra clothes, and Poppa would prepare a gift for the occasion, but someone always forgot something important.

Then the entire family, like a small army troop armed with bags and boxes, would hurry to the trolley stop. The trolley ride was the first of many exciting rides the family would take that day. At the East River ferry slip, the family boarded a delightful steam-powered ferryboat bound east along Connecticut's coastline. Willi fondly remembered standing at the rail, letting the breezes blow through her hair. She imagined herself a sailor: Long Island Sound the exotic Pacific, and the ferry, a steamer bound for China. For the better part of a day, the family enjoyed the excursion and Mama's picnic lunch served on the open deck. By late afternoon the steamer voyage was over and everyone, tired but still excited, clamored onto a small city wharf hours from home.

Mama and Poppa always got nervous as the ferry docked. Willi remembered that Mama was sure they would miss their train, but the enormous engine and its train of cars always seemed to know when they would arrive at the dock. *Maybe it was waiting just for us*, Willi reasoned as they hurried towards their seats in the parlor cars. The engine's boiler began to release long deafening bursts of steam, a sign that the train was ready to move, and it always lurched forward before they were safely seated.

The noisy train was uncomfortably packed with travelers, but Willi never seemed to remember the train rides. She'd sit down, put her duffle on the bench, and within minutes the swaying of the rail car lulled her into dreamland. It always seemed to happen this way, even when she willed it differently.

What Willi did remember, though, was being awakened by the ear-splitting squeals of metal on metal as the train jerked and swayed to a stop. Half awake, half asleep, she waited for that loud release of steam that signaled the car was totally stopped. Little Sophie always screamed at the noise and violent jerks of the train car; Mama never seemed able to quiet her when this happened. Willi didn't know why Mama's ways didn't work here, but when this happened, Mama got such an odd look on her face and she seemed just a little less like their Mama. It was unsettling and when this happened Willi worried more about her mother than Sophie.

"Oh, Grandpa," Beth would call and wave at a heavily built man on a huge lumber wagon pulled by the most handsome team of horses on earth. "Over here. We're over here."

Feeling guilty, Willi always wondered which she wanted to see first, Grandpa Marten or his horses.

But today was not summer and she and Beth, and all the other children were still here in New York and Poppa had been gone almost a week. Maybe Beth was right, she should be afraid.

At breakfast that morning, Mama had been especially cheerful.

"Children," she said, "tonight Poppa will be home." Everyone, even baby Dottie and little Sophie, let out a collective cheer, but they could all see how relieved Mama was with the news. However, by suppertime Poppa was not home and Mama was beginning to lose her cheerfulness.

"If Poppa said he was coming home today," Beth said, "then Poppa will be home. He always keeps his word."

That was hours ago and now Willi turned over and faced the open window. From here, she would be able to hear the screech of the trolley as is turned the corner at the foot of their street.

I must stay awake. I must see Poppa tonight. I can't sleep until I know that Poppa is safely home. The words repeated over and over in her mind while the soft breeze through the open window piped a tune for the night shadows that now danced in Willi's dreams.

"Willi, Willi, wake up little sister," Beth coaxed Willi awake. "Sssh, don't make any noise, but come with me." The girls hurried from the attic bedroom to the hallway stairs. "Poppa is home and he and Mama are having fresh coffee and talking, right now, in the middle of the night."

Willi tingled all over. It was even more exciting than Christmas when they had tried to wait up for Santa. The sisters tiptoed toward the shaft of kitchen light and the hushed voices that flowed into the hallway through the almost-closed door.

"Over here, girls," a whispered voice called to them and there in a safe shadow was William. Quickly, the girls joined their brother under the stairway.

"What have they said? What did you hear?" queried Beth.

"Well, I know this," William's words of wisdom were deliberate and carefully chosen. "I heard the trolley stop and Poppa come into the kitchen. That's when I came down here so I could watch them, secretly. Mama was waiting for him; I don't think she ever went to bed. Anyway, they talked for a moment then Mama put on a fresh pot of coffee. She never does that at this hour of the night!"

"Look!" Willi tugged on their nightclothes for attention. As the trio watched, Poppa took his sketchbook out of his duffle and pulled his chair up close to Mama. Carefully he opened to a drawing and the two of them followed as he pointed out markings on the page. Poppa's words were soft and as he finished he looked Mama squarely in the eyes and took her hands in his.

"Oh no!"

Beth could not contain herself any longer, "Mama's crying! Mama almost never cries. I just know something terrible has happened."

Slightly off balance on her hallway perch and tilting towards the kitchen to hear, Beth suddenly felt her body moving. Willi grabbed for her sister's robe, but it was too late. Beth fell towards the shaft of kitchen light and with a crashing thud, burst through the doorway to make a spectacular entrance onto the kitchen floor.

Still clinging desperately to Beth's robe, Willi tumbled forward through the open door, crumpling across her sister's fallen body. Not wishing to miss one moment of this sudden action, William bolted through the doorway and valiantly stepped across his sisters' sprawled bodies to captain the children's secret brigade.

Mama and Poppa starred in disbelief at the circus on their kitchen floor.

It was late, very late when Willi and Beth finally returned to their attic bedroom. There were no moon shadows now, just the whistle of a light breeze in the branches outside. The girls were too excited to talk and soon the breeze lulled them towards a dream-filled sleep. Soon there would be a trip to the country like none other they'd ever taken before. This time they would stay forever on the new farm that Poppa had purchased. Everyone had gazed at the pictures Poppa had drawn and touched the soil and dust that remained on his hat. No wonder Mama had cried; they had all cried with joy at the thought of this wonderful adventure.

But in Mama's bedroom, little Sophie lay on the bed, her body jerking with convulsions. The excitement of the evening had been too much for the child. Mama carefully cradled Sophie's head in her hands, stroked her hair and cheeks until the seizures quieted. Kristine sat quietly until little Sophie had drifted off into a deep sleep and once again, as it had been in the earliest days of Sophie's illness, Mama felt the toll that Sophie was taking on her body and soul. Slowly but surely, both were being torn apart.

"Oh Lord," she said. "Is this how you have chosen to help us? Is this your answer to my prayers?" She reached to pick up her glasses and turn off the gaslight that illuminated the child's room, but her hands fell instead on the small prayer book of her mother's. Out of habit she opened the book and read the first line that caught her eye: "*And there shall be a hiding place from the wind, and a covert from the tempest, as rivers of water in a dry place, as the shadow of a great rock in a weary land.*"

A Hiding Place From The Wind

Part Three: The Hiding Place

Moving Day

The day after Rob returned home, two things happened: the moving date was set and Kristine began her campaign.

"Rob," she began, "We need to use a professional moving company. The Robbson's moved many times while I worked for them; their things were always safe and arrived in good shape."

"Kristine, the Robbson's are wealthy, we don't have that kind of money. No, that's out of the question! Beside, yesterday I talked to Rawson at the office and he suggested some friends of Marten's, the ones that moved him up to the country some years ago. They quoted me an affordable price and I told them their offer was generous, so I hired them."

Kristine bristled at the thought that he'd made the decision without even talking to her. She tried once more to make her point. "Don't you remember the problems Marten had with that move? Those movers didn't show up on time, pieces of furniture were broken and things were missing."

"Those things happen in a move, you expect it."

Kristine had one last hand to play. "And don't you remember that when they finally arrived at Marten's, the truck cab was littered with whiskey bottles and one of the men was drunk?"

Rob stiffened and swung about to face his wife. Kristine could see the anger deep in his eyes and almost instantly his demeanor changed from conversational to resolve. Kristine knew she had touched a tender nerve. "I don't want to talk about that day. They were good men, hard workers. It's just that whiskey brings out the demon in decent men. They do things they don't even remember, bad things. I'd have the sale of whiskey banned if the Lord would show me how. I hate what the Devil's drink does to reasonable men." Rob, finished with his flash of self-righteousness, returned to the task at hand, but Kristine knew by his quiet intense work that he was deeply engaged in thought, searching for a way to overcome this newly presented barrier.

"I know what to do," he said suddenly. "I'll tell them if I so much as smell whiskey or see a bottle they won't be paid the balance of the job. I'll make it a condition of the move." Rob was adamant that the family's move from New York to Connecticut would be on his terms and under his direction, not his wife's, and certainly not his father's. "Rawson also told me," Rob added, "that he'd drive the family to Marten's farm and wouldn't charge us for the trip. Said he had lumber company business to do with Marten, so the company would pay for the auto trip to Connecticut. The drive will take a full day and we'll spend the night with Marten and Hanna. In the morning, everyone can travel out to our new home and meet the moving truck."

Almost immediately after arriving home, Rob had begun the task of making crates. Using his woodworking skills, he measured up the items to be moved and built wooden boxes to match their sizes. All manner of goods filled those multi-sized chests, including a full service of bone china Mrs. Robbson had sent them as a wedding gift, several Tiffany lamps; and items of decorative glassware. There were wall tapestries and impressively framed oil paintings, including one of a giant elk who's oddly painted eyes haunted Willi. She was sure that the elk's eyes were watching her every movement, no matter where the painting hung. Then of course there were Rob's office contents: his drawings, tools, and drafting furniture.

Preparing to move an entire household took weeks of preparation and hours and hours of hard work. Every day new challenges presented themselves, but the Johnson family was determined to make this herculean effort a family affair. While Rob and Kristine did the bulk of the work, everyone from their oldest son to their youngest daughter was to be a part in this life-changing experience.

Moving is a physical task but it is also a mental task. In the process of sifting through the accumulation of material goods, of discarding items and choosing to keep others, we touch moments in our life's story. These pauses of remembrance can generate microburst of anguish or gentle breezes of delight.

"Mama, tell me once again about the mandolin," said Beth. It was her afternoon to help with the packing and a chance to spend time alone with her mother.

Kristine picked up the instrument and ran her hand over the polished wood. She fingered the strings. "My father played an instrument like this one when I was a child. I loved to sit and listen to the music. When I worked for the Robbsons I was able to save enough to buy this instrument and one of my friends taught me how to play. I loved playing and soon I joined a string band with some of my Swedish co-workers. We'd gather on our days off to play together and learn new tunes. There were lots of young people at these gatherings and that's where I first met your father. He didn't play an instrument but he liked listening to the music. Beth, those were such good times but it was so long ago."

"Play me a tune Mama, please."

Kristine's fingers obligingly picked a short but lively dance tune. As the last note lingered in the air, her hands remained on the instrument as if awaiting permission to pick yet another tune, but Kristine's reason prevailed. "That's enough for today, Beth. I'll pack it in this box and it'll be safe." Kristine placed the instrument on a soft comforter within one of the crates, and then covered it with a second quilt just as soft as the first. Protecting the mandolin was important, not just for the joy that the music provided, but because it embodied Kristine's youthful dreams. Those joyful times still lived within the mandolin.

Then there was the airplane. The entire family had become fascinated by the new phenomena called flying machines; many of those intriguing machines were housed in the small airfields that dotted the Long Island countryside. Every day the family had a front row seat to watch those planes cavort and frolic in the air above their home.

One evening after the children had recounted a particularly lively day of flyers above the house, Poppa surprised everyone. "You know, I could build a plane. Well, for starters, I could build a model plane."

"Yes, yes! Can you Poppa? Please, build us a plane." The children's cries were unanimous.

Working in his spare time, Rob began his plane-building task. The flyer took months to build, but when it was done, the model was perfect in every detail. Kristine carefully covered the plane's wooden frame with silk from one of Mrs. Robbson's old dresses and then proudly painted it blue and gold. The plane, stunning from every angle, was a genuine masterpiece. At some point in its construction everyone in the family had helped to make this magical plane—even little Sophie had dabbed with the paintbrush. It truly had become a family project, so it was with real fanfare that the family gathered around to watch Mama pack the plane. She carefully lifted the model and placed it on a soft blanket inside a sturdy crate. The voids around the plane were carefully stuffed with chintz curtains, and then finally, an upside-down box was secured on top of the plane to keep it from being crushed. Like the rest of the family's precious treasures, the plane was properly packed and ready for the movers.

It didn't take long for the crates to be filled, so old steamer trunks—sturdy reminders of ocean crossings—now reappeared from the attic. Rob arranged them around the walls of the parlor. They could now be filled in a logical order.

In the spirit of family cooperation, Kristine had enlisted the children's help in carrying a variety of items from the upstairs rooms to the parlor. "Children, you can start carrying the linens downstairs now. Be careful on the stairs and don't try to carry too many at one time." Kristine's call for items to pack resulted in a ragtag parade of children up and down the stairs. Each trip brought armloads of bedding, curtains, and pillows. It seemed an endless task. The children worked diligently and Kristine packed trunk after trunk until the children had had enough and fatigue began to overcome reasonableness and discipline.

"Let's cover up William," someone said in jest, but the girls immediately thought it a splendid idea, and a comforter was promptly dropped on their unsuspecting brother.

"This is better than a snowdrift," Beth giggled and piled another load on her brother, who was now hidden under the soft cotton mound. Sensing something special was happening, Sophie, in pure Sophie-talk, began ordering the attack on William and little Dottie gleefully followed her sister into battle. All the children had now flung themselves into the pile of bedclothes in an all out assault on their brother.

"Stop this tomfoolery right now!" Kristine's sharp voice cut through the laughter, but for once it did little good. She stepped closer, reaching down to pull Dottie away from the commotion, but instead her feet slid on the linens and she fell into the gigantic mound of children, pillows, and bed linens. Without warning, Kristine suddenly felt herself breaking, coming apart from deep inside her total being. This was the last straw. All the stress of moving, running a household, meeting Rob's demands and corralling the children in these difficult days was taking its toll. Sprawled across the mound of linens and bedclothes, cathartic laughter rose from deep with the women who for too long had checked and controlled all her emotions. Unbridled laughter flooded her total being and suddenly she felt like a different woman, one that had been hiding for far too long. The freedom and joy of childish play bubbled up from somewhere deep within and her stress and anxiety began to vanish with each roll of laughter. "Oh my, I hope your father doesn't come in and see the mess we've made," she said as she drew herself into a respectable posture. The normally proper Mama then reached out and playfully tousled her son's hair, tossed a pillow towards the girls and tickled her two youngest until they giggled uncontrollably. She smiled, *No, Rob just wouldn't understand, but it feels so good.*

Packing the rigid old steamer trunks was not as easy as packing the crates. The crates had to be nailed closed when full, but the trunks had locks and clasps. Kristine filled the last of the trunks as full as she could and lowered the slightly curved lid down upon its contents. The trunk wouldn't close. She pushed down on the contents that yielded slightly to her effort, but the lid was still far from the clasps.

"William, Beth! Come and help me close this trunk." Mama rearranged some of the items inside and then the children pushed down on the top lid with all their strength. The lid was closer to the clasp, but would not catch.

"William, sit on the lid," Beth suggested, but the trunk still wouldn't close.

"Hey Willi," William called out to his sister. "Help us!" Finally, with one more push, Kristine was able to snap the clasps closed.

Finally the packing was done and the movers arrived to load their truck. Rob was hawkeyed in his supervision of their work.

"Careful with those crates boys, you're handling them too roughly." Rob oversaw and directed the loading of the entire household. He even wrote FRAGILE in large red letters on the topside of several crates and pointed out those crates that needed even more care. "These two crates," he called to the crew's foreman, "are especially fragile. They need to be handled gently and placed where they won't be crushed."

The foreman, already annoyed with Rob's interference, retorted, "Why, what's so special about those boxes? Probably some kind of fancy glass or dishes. We know how to handle those things."

"These are not house wares. That one," Rob pointed towards one of two marked crates, "has a model airplane that the family built, and the other has Kristine's mandolin. They are important to the family."

By dawn the next day, the mover's truckload had passed Rob's final inspection and pulled away from the Hunt Street house. Rob then turned his attention to his family, assisting them as they arranged themselves and their precious treasures in the huge nine-passenger auto. He would follow them, riding to Connecticut with his brother John, who at the last minute had also agreed to make the trip.

"Kristine, It will take me a couple of hours to close up the house and settle affairs here, then I'll be off with John. We'll follow the same route as you, so if there is trouble remember we'll be along shortly. I'm sure you'll be safe with Rawson." He turned to the children, "See you tonight, have a good trip."

"Rob," Rawson laughed, "look at this motley crew! Am I driving a fine auto or an open tin can of tightly packed sardines?"

Rawson had a point. Even though the Packard was one of the finest autos of its day, it didn't have a hard-sided passenger compartment. The auto was meant for touring, so it had carriage-style window curtains that attached to the auto's fabric top. When not secured in place, this window design gave little protection against the weather, so the entire family had donned winter coats and scarves. There was no extra room to be had anywhere in the car.

"Connecticut or bust!" Rawson exclaimed and released the brake. The car moved down the Hunt Street hill and the journey was underway.

Even though it was a beautiful spring day, the air was still cold and Rawson hadn't wanted to close the car's windows, but Kristine had had enough of the children's complaining. "Mr. Rawson, I know you love your car and you're dressed for all this open air driving, but the windows need to be closed. Tomorrow these children will all be sick with ear aches if that cold wind isn't blocked right now, and if I have anything to say about it, and I will, you'll be the person who sits and cares for them as they cry." Rawson pulled the car over, closed the window curtains and the trek continued on its way.

The children were delighted that the trip was actually underway, but within several hours fatigue started to overtake everyone.

"Mama, William's taking too much of the seat. He's pushing me."

"I'm not. Beth's got too much on her lap, tell her to put it on the floor."

"I can't, Willi's got all her treasures there."

"Mama, I'm cold."

Kristine handed Willi a woolen scarf, "Wrap this around your neck, it should help."

"Mama can you stop Sophie from making those awful noises?"

"Just ignore it, William." Mama replied.

"Well, can she stop bouncing on the seat?"

"Just calm down, I'll hold her on my lap, maybe that will help."

As the miles rolled on, the children eventually settled down, their heads nodded, and finally their eyes closed. A boring monotony overtook the travelers. Even Mr. Rawson's gruff comments were stilled.

Bang, fa-lop, fa-lop, fa-lop, screech

"Mr. Rawson, what is that noise? Is something wrong with the car?" The car swerved uncontrollably and bounced towards the uneven shoulder at the side of the road. "Oh, dear God," Kristine cried, "We're going into to crash into that rock."

"Dag blast it! Flat tire." Rawson wrestled the bolting vehicle to a safe stop. "Everyone out! Got to change the tire."

The trip proved to be exhausting, the good nature of the driver and passengers all wilted as the day progressed. The blown tire was the first of two, then a stop for fuel and physical relief so that by the time they stopped for a late roadside lunch, Rob and his brother John had caught up with them. Kristine suddenly felt safer and the children squealed with delight at the sight of their father.

* * * * * * * *

"So Kristine how was it with all the children on such a long ride?" Hanna asked as they cleared the dishes from the dinner table. Hanna and Martin had made the weary travelers welcome with a warm meal and friendly company. Normally Mama wouldn't have said much about the trip, but tonight it almost felt good to tell some tales.

"The children were terrible fussy Hanna, all of them, but Sophie was the worst. She sat on my lap the entire way. Honestly, I thought my arm would fall off from holding her so tightly. She squirmed and cried, tried to escape from my arms and talked her Sophie-talk the entire way. Mr. Rawson was becoming terribly annoyed and I was sure he would stop at any moment and tell us to get out and walk. I'm sad to say that the closer we got to your home the sharper I got with the children, until I'm sure they believed me to be the ogre of their fairy tale stories."

"Tomorrow's trip to your new farm isn't as long," Hanna said. "There aren't many dinner dishes left. Put that towel down now and go to bed. You've had a hard day, so go on now and get a good night's sleep."

The New Home Awaits

A parade of vehicles picked their way through and around the lingering spring ruts that dotted the gravel road. Marten's old farm truck led the procession, followed by Rawson's Packard filled with the anxious and excited family. The moving truck lumbered along slowly and at the end of the rag-tag procession was a group of Marten's friends, anxious to be helpful. For a road that rarely saw a handful of vehicles in a week, this procession was indeed an exceptional sight.

At the last minute Rob's brother John decided to stay on to help with the move. "Rob, Hanna said she'll ride with the children in Rawson's car, so why don't you and Kristine ride out to the new farm with me? It might be more relaxing for Kristine, yesterday was a hard travel day for her."

Passengers loaded, John's truck pulled into the processional line. The brothers chatted about family matters but Kristine rode silently not listening to their conversation; her gaze was fixated on the landscape and her thoughts began to roil by what she saw. About a half hour down the road Kristine suddenly broke her silence. "Rob, why are there so many fields that seem neglected? The farm buildings that I can see from the road don't look inhabited; are you sure this was a good decision?"

"Well, Marten told me some of the history about this part of town. Seems that the western portion was the last of the town to be surveyed and deeded to settlers. The more fertile portions of the town were built up and settled first, but after more families came from England and Massachusetts, the town needed more land. So that opened up this portion to settlement."

"There are so many rocks and boulders. I can see them there in the forest, in places where the trees aren't as thick. This land will be very hard to farm, if not impossible." The landscape wasn't bolstering Kristine's confidence.

"Well, I also heard that many of the Englishmen's farms in this part of the town were failures. It was just too hard to make a living or grow enough crops to support a reasonable size farm. Those settlers just gave up and started again somewhere else, usually in a neighboring town."

The pair rode on in silence, each absorbed in their own thoughts. Goaded by Kristine's words, Rob recalled the words of the auctioneer on the day of the sale. "Out here you're on your own. There are some neighbors, but more abandoned farms than working ones. Real glad you have some family here. Locals like to keep to themselves, they're not unkind, just wary of strangers." Those words sat heavy on Rob's shoulders. He believed Kristine felt them, too.

"Kristine," Rob broke the silence. "Our little valley isn't like the land you've been seeing along this roadside. Our home is in a small fertile valley. There's a good source of water close by in a stream and open fields with good soil. Our fields aren't badly overgrown, as they've been farmed recently. There is forestland, but not too much. We have neighbors close by, at least three farms we can almost see and several just a short drive away. When the weather dries out and travel on the roads is easier, Marten and the family won't seem so far away."

Though Kristine felt somewhat reassured by Rob's comments, she also knew that this was his first journey of migration. Long ago her first move had been from the small village of her childhood to a large bustling city. It had been an exciting time, a new beginning. Now she sensed that excitement within Rob. He wanted this move to work out. No matter how blustery he might be on occasion, he loved his family and this sacrifice had been made for all of them, but especially for little Sophie and William. Kristine realized that moving as many times as she had changed her perspective. Each time her moves pushed her forward to a better life, a more modern life, and closer to achieving her dreams of an American life. So why did today feel so different? Was she moving forward or backward? All she knew for sure was that there was no turning back.

As they neared the farm, Kristine believed no one would even know they had arrived. She was wrong.

The Harris' owned one of those neighboring farms that you could almost see from the Johnson's new home. As was the farming tradition of the times, Selma had just served her husband and their hired hand their second breakfast. As she glanced out her kitchen window she noticed unusual activity on the roadway beyond their western pasture. A procession of vehicles was slowly making its way toward the old Chamberlain farm.

"New neighbors arriving," she remarked to her husband and his hired hand, then turned back to watch. "Never thought I'd see another family down there. Lord, do they know how bad that house is? It should have been knocked down and burned."

The month of May had given the family a perfect spring day to make their move, but sometimes the brighter the sunshine, the less one sees.

Reality

The old Chamberlain farm already had a history when the Johnson's bought the property in 1920. Originally settled in the 1700s, it had expanded and changed many times during the 200 years before their purchase. Its original owners were now buried in a neighboring graveyard and its deed had been re-written numerous times. Chamberlain had simply been its most recent owner. The original acreage of the farm had once been large, but by 1920 when the Johnson's bought it, only 88 acres remained. The farmhouse remained an antique primitive residence and the farm's outbuildings adequate for only a subsistence farm. The property contained no modern amenities and it was situated a considerable distance from the closest center of commerce. The farmstead required its inhabitants to be highly self-sufficient.

In their efforts to make a more positive life for their family, Rob and Kristine had unwittingly undertaken a task more demanding than any they had encountered before. While they were intelligent and resourceful people, their expectations for a smooth and successful change of place in which to conduct life as usual would prove to be impossible. The physical and emotional skills they possessed would prove to be woefully inadequate for the task at hand.

Kristine's Story
(Kristine recalls the challenges of those first days)

Rob had told me in detail, at least three times over, everything that he could remember about the new home. So as Rawson's Packard made the last turn towards the house I silently prayed that I would find few surprises. I didn't know why, but something within me was overly cautious.

At first, the new farm looked like a Valhalla of sorts. The lay of the farmland was beautiful, just as Rob had described. The hills surrounding our valley were densely forested, forming a barrier against the rest of the world, but the bowl of the valley was open with rolling fields and a stream at the margin of the pastureland. Once the car stopped, the children immediately scattered to explore the large hay barn and open fields. Fresh air, sunshine and a bright May greening was all that they needed to feel liberated, but Rob's and my attention was drawn towards the house. Almost immediately that sense of foreboding returned.

It had been more than a month since Rob had been here with Marten. Someone had told me that on the day of the auction the remaining inhabitants of the household had simply gathered a few personal items and walked away from the house. I had no idea what to expect.

Rob pushed the kitchen door open. It swung inward allowing the sunshine to illuminate the room. Never in all my life had I beheld such a devastating array of clutter and squalor. I felt a ripple of disgust sweep over me as rats scurried away towards their raceways in the ceilings and walls, leaving well-worn trails across every visible surface. Instantly I realized that when the people moved out the rats moved in, and for more than a month those rodents had been devouring every edible item left behind.

Even with the door open and light pouring in, the room beyond the doorway was dark and reeked with the smell of kerosene. I could see a kitchen range across the room, but its stovepipe, barely attached to the chimney, threatened to collapse onto to the floor at any moment. Black streaks of creosote flowed downward from the stovepipe and stained the dirty, loose wallpaper. Filthy rags stuffed numerous cracks and holes. My heart sank in dismay.

"Oh my Lord! Rob, did those people really live here? How could they live in this filth?"

Rob, equally shocked at the sight, tried to make light of the situation. "Kristine, I'm sure the rest of the house is better. The place just needs a good cleaning, some fresh paint, and bright new wallpaper. Come on, let's take a look at the rest of the rooms."

Rob carefully stepped through the doorway into the keeping room, a sort of primitive kitchen, but he hadn't taken more than a few steps across the floor when I heard a groaning from beneath the floorboards. Suddenly a loud cracking sound filled the room and I watched in horror as an entire section of the kitchen floor collapsed, swallowing Rob in one gigantic gulp.

I was terrified and began screaming at Rob and for anyone that could hear me. Those screams sure must have been loud, as Marten and his friends came running, unsure of what ungodly event had just taken place. I stood there, unable to say even one word; my hands frozen to the doorframe, my heart beating so hard I thought it would simply jump right out of my chest. All I could do was point to the huge black hole.

"Rob, Rob? Can you hear me?" Rob's brother kept shouting his name but there was no answer. "Get a light. Can anyone find a ladder?"

Marten came running with a large light that he promptly shone down into the hole. "I see him laying face down in the dirt with boards and a beam across his back."

I remember one of Marten's friends jumped into the hole and carefully lifted the debris off Rob's back. Then there was silence. Finally Marten's friend reappeared.

"That fall knocked the wind out of him and a little daylight too, but I don't think any bones are broken. Boy, is he going to be hurting tomorrow. Give me a hand to get him out of this hole. It's wet and cold down here, and smells right musty too."

I had a hard time regaining my composure, but I was so glad to see Rob pulled out of that hole. Covered in muck and mud, dirty and with a ripped shirt, my husband had never looked as wonderful as he did at that moment, and thankfully beyond some cuts and bruises, he wasn't seriously hurt. Right about then I realized that there was no way that we were going to move into this house, at least not today.

The movers had found a couple of chairs, removed them from the truck and set them on the lawn. It felt good to sit down, as my legs were still shaky. The children had all gathered around me by now, worried about their father and what would happen next. Sophie and Dottie didn't know what to make of their shaken mother, so they just held onto my legs, making it impossible for me to get up. Rob was up and walking around almost immediately, though I saw that he favored his right leg slightly. He spent a good bit of time talking with his father and the other men, but after a bit he came back and sat down beside me.

"Rob, what are we going to do? This house is unlivable. I expected problems, but maybe this place was just one terrible mistake." I could feel the tears well up in my eyes.

"Marten and Hanna have invited us to stay at their farm while we decide how to solve this problem. That would be best for everybody. Tomorrow things won't seem so bad and then we'll make a plan. The men will unload the truck into the barn and we'll bring some perishable items back to Marten's." Rob reached down and took my hands in his. He looked me straight in the eyes and said with complete conviction, "The Lord led us here to this place, to our farm. I know he'll help us now. He'll help us find a way around these difficulties, of that I'm sure."

During the next several weeks the shock of the first day began to wear off and I began to see the farm in a fresh light. To be sure it would be a challenge—a massive challenge, and one I hoped I had the strength and courage to endure—but I watched the children as they discovered the animals, explored the gigantic hay barn, ran in the greening grass, and were happier than I had ever seen them, especially Sophie. So, as a family we began the task of making those crumbling walls and dilapidated buildings into our home, one-step at a time.

Rob was able to buy a huge war surplus tent. We staked it down tightly in the space between the house and barn. Then the children and I assembled a bivouac kitchen of sorts. It was a place to cook, eat, and get out of the rain, wind, and sun. While the children and I began the formidable task of cleaning the rest of the house, which as Rob had suspected was not as rotten as the kitchen, he and William attacked the task of repairing the worst portions of the house. Rob made a plan about what was essential to fix right away and what could wait for a while, and then ordered materials from the lumberyard in New York. While they waited for the order's arrival, he and William worked with a vengeance, pulling out the worst of the rotted material and clearing the work area of debris. I believe Rob was intent on proving that he hadn't made a huge mistake by making the house habitable in record time.

"Morning folks!" Marten's booming voice announced his arrival even before he'd stepped down off the wagon. "Special delivery from my private lumberyard."

"Marten," I called out, "what speedy service. Why, it has hardly been a week since you placed that order."

"Rob's brother Nat will be here soon with a second wagonload, then some of the boys from the church plan to stop by and help unload the wagons. For now though, does that fancy kitchen of yours have a hot cup of coffee?"

By day's end, all the building materials had been unloaded and stacked. Some of the men who came to help told Rob they'd come by when they could and give him a hand, and they did. Before too long, the most critical work was completed and the children could move from the hayloft to the attic of the house.

We still had so much work to do that at times it seemed overwhelming, but one day the girls and I decided to unpack the remaining crates and boxes. It was exciting as each of the boxes was opened. It really hadn't been that long since we carefully packed away the contents of our old home, but it seemed as if it was an eternity.

"Mama," Willi called out excitedly. "I didn't lose my pencil box. Someone must have found it and slipped it into this box."

I admit it was like Christmas seeing our beautiful things again. "Now girls, a peek is all we can have today. They are safe in the crates as we have no place to put them right now."

"Mama," Beth called to me, excited to see just a little more, "I want to see the mandolin and airplane. Let's look for those crates."

Beth rummaged through the stack of crates then suddenly stopped. "Mama, something's wrong. Come here and look." She pointed to the fasteners on the top of the crate, "These have already been opened."

My heart sank as we opened first one crate, then the other.

"Oh, Mama, they're gone. The mandolin and the plane aren't here, they're both missing." Beth began to cry, then suddenly all the children were crying. I couldn't believe it but rather than crying, I could feel myself getting angry, really angry. I tore into the packaging materials, but it was of little use, there was nothing there. They were gone. Accepting this loss was so hard to understand. Why, why would they do that? Why would they take those items? Was it because Rob had pressed the movers so hard about not drinking on the job, or was it simply that there is always a price to pay for a bargain fee? Whatever the reason, our precious things never made it to Connecticut and it was the only problem I never let Rob forget.

When I look back at those beginnings, it seems impossible to believe that this groaning ancient structure and unkempt but beautiful plot of land would become the most precious spot on earth to me, but it did. It became a magical place, my American Dream come true... but that would not happen for many, many years. There was so much work to do, so much living to endure, and too many times when I felt the task was impossible. We'd been through so much and now we had a chance for everyone to thrive, not just some of us. When Rob became discouraged, when our money was at an end or there were unexpected needs, I would tell everyone, "Let's go take another look at the bottom of the barrel. I'm sure there is something in there that we can scrape off the sides to make it work." And somehow, there always seemed to be something there.

But at night, when I was alone and the fears and challenges threatened to overwhelm me, I'd hold my Mama's little prayer book, its cover now bent and its pages dog-eared and ragged, and thank the Lord for guiding our path, for sustaining us, and not giving up on us—even when our best efforts failed and we had to turn around and try a different road.

On a Farm, Even a Little One, Everyone Works

It took several trips and most of the morning, but by the mid-day meal, Rob's brother Nat had returned all the family's animals to the Johnson's barn. Kristine set an extra plate and the hungry farmer joined them.

"Rob, I got bad news for you. That red and white cow you bought is sick. Don't exactly know what's wrong, probably started when old Chamberlain owned her and didn't take care of her. Anyway, now she's a really sick cow. Kept her separated from my cows while you were gone and hoped she'd get better, but she hasn't. She really needs a veterinarian to come and take a look at her."

Nat continued, "The other one, the Holstein is okay, but she's dry. No milk for the family from this herd. Sorry to bring you that news, Rob."

Rob hadn't planned on this turn of events. A sick milk cow, that was bad. The family desperately needed milk and he'd counted on that cow to provide it.

"So, what about the other animals, the horse, the chickens? How are they?"

"Well, don't know how soon the chickens will start laying again, but some good feed might help. And the horse, he's a real beauty, but you'll have to learn how he handles. He's blind in the left eye so always come up on him from the right side, then he's okay, but if you surprise him from the left he'll kick out at you real bad and even bolt if he's being driven. Once he knows you're working on him, like harnessing him up and recognizes that you're handling him, he's fine. Just be careful approaching him and keep surprises away. He a really good worker and drives great."

****

The next day the traveling farm vet showed up in his old truck. "Been out to Marten Johansson's this morning and he told me you had an ailing cow. Thought I'd swing by to take a look at her. Most animals don't show any problems, but the longer they are infected the more likely they are to lose weight, be lethargic, and cough a lot."

"That's exactly how my brother said she was acting, especially the cough."

The vet continued, "Good, we'll test both cows. TB is a real problem these days; hope that's not the case here. Are the cows out in the pasture or still in the barn, Rob?"

"They're up in the barn. Hadn't turned the animals out yet."

The vet continued, "I need to give them a skin test then come back in a day or two and check on the needle site. The shot is called a tine test, and is actually a mild injection of the tuberculosis bacteria. How the cow's body reacts to the test determines if the animal is infected."

The vet prepared the test needles and proceeded to test both cows. He picked up each cow's tail and pricked the sensitive skin in that protected region. Then he made a mark next to the needle prick so he could easily find the injection site. "There, that's done. I'll be back to measure the lump the test will produce. The size of the lump will determine if either of them is infected or not. Meanwhile, keep the animals separated."

Two days later the vet returned to look at the injection sites. He tested the red cow first by measuring the large lump with a special ruler and strange markings. A rather large lump had grown at the prick site. Rob watched the vet's face and knew even before the doctor spoke the outcome of the test on his sick cow.

"Bad news, Rob, and not a great way to start your life here. The size of the lump on the red milk cow means that she has the disease and has to be put down. It's the law. The Holstein heifer is healthy, no growth at all from the test. Tuberculosis in cattle and wild animals is a real problem. They can easily infect a herd and other animals, but for sure she's carrying a really dangerous disease that the government wants to control. Her milk is unsafe to drink unless it's pasteurized. Maybe your milk was pasteurized in the city, but out here without electricity it's hard unless you sell to a dairy." The vet looked around the farm, then surprised Rob by saying, "You do know that the cow's meat doesn't need to go to waste. Why not slaughter her here on the farm, dig a burial hole for her but leave it so the those scrawny chickens can eat off the carcass for a few days?"

Rob knew Kristine would never knowingly let diseased meat or milk into her kitchen. She was foot-down against that, rather waste it than get someone sick, but if the chickens could safely eat the meat, at least the cow wouldn't be a complete waste. "Can we do the deed now? No sense putting it off."

Rob and the vet led the cow to the far end of the lane, stopping near the wood lot entrance. Rob handed the farm's only rifle to the vet. The vet took the rifle, aimed at the back of the cow's head and with one shot felled the red cow to the ground.

"I know it's necessary," Rob said to the vet, "but I hate the killing part of living. My boy and I will be back later and dig the hole. For now though, we'll just let her be."

That night at the supper table, everyone wanted to know what had happened. *Decision time*, Rob realized. "Eat your supper and after everyone is done, we'll talk about what happened today."

For once the family willingly remained at the table. Kristine cleared the supper dishes, poured a cup of coffee for both she and Rob and then sat down.

"Children, today everyone saw the vet came to check on our sick cow." Rob began. "She was very sick and suffering. She could have made us all sick, too."

He thought hard about what he was going to say next, and then continued.

"Life out here in the country can be hard. We sometimes have to make decisions we'd rather not make, but those decisions are for everyone's good. So the vet took care of the red cow and now she can't spread her disease to us or the other animals."

"You mean he killed her." Beth said.

"Yes Beth, she died, and Grandpa Marten is going to bring over one of his cows for us until I can buy a new milk cow." He wasn't going to tell them about what would happen to her meat. "Now, let me tell you about our horse."

Willi couldn't wait one minute more. "Poppa, Poppa, I named the horse. His name is Buster and I already asked him if he likes it. I think he does."

"Well, you've got to be really careful with Buster, then. The horse is blind on his left side."

"I know! I know, Poppa. Uncle Nat told me. You have to come at him from the right side and talk to him very gently. Oh, I love that horse."

Poppa smiled and sighed. *Oh, Willi*, he thought, *before long you'll want to live in the barn with all the animals.*

He turned to little Dottie. "And which of the animals do you like best?"

"Poppa, I like the chickens."

Kristine spoke up, "Dottie and I are going to take care of the chickens. She already started looking for their eggs."

"Poppa," Dottie added with an unusual excitement, "Mama says they like to hide their eggs, so it's like an egg hunt everyday. That's my job Poppa, helping Mama with the chickens."

Poor Poppa, instead of being in charge of assigning farm chores, the children had already taken over. At least his son had said nothing, yet.

"William, what have you decided needs your help?"

"Oh, Poppa, that's easy. There's so much equipment here, and it all needs some fixing. I want to work on the mechanical stuff and maybe I can get the parts and make a radio so we know what is going on in the world, and *maybe*…" He loudly emphasized the word and paused, "…we could find an old truck to buy. I can learn to drive. It's not hard, really."

"The Captain of Transportation – yup, that will be your job; but for now, transportation is of the horse powered, four-legged variety."

Poppa knew someday they'd have mechanical power, but for now they had to work with what they had, and William already knew how to handle horses. When there are too few hands to go around, one learns a lot at a very young age.

"You might start looking around at the equipment we have and see how useable it is. I know we have a wagon and a buggy; I'm not sure what else is here. Marten will deliver some supplies to us, but we've got to use that horse if we want to do anything for ourselves. Most things are just too heavy for us to lift or pull… we'll need that horse for muscle and brute force. There are harnesses and such in the barn and I hope they are all useable."

"Poppa," Willi interrupted. "William and I already checked that out. William said there's at least one full driving harness and several work collars." Willi had memorized William's words, but honestly, the little girl had no idea what she was talking about. Poppa laughed, but then she added, "If I help him I can learn more, Poppa. Please say I can." Rob smiled and nodded knowing that it didn't make a difference what he said, as she'd just do it anyway.

Rob turned to his oldest daughter. "Beth, Mama needs you in the kitchen and house so that'll be your main chore. Willi, you'll be in charge of Sophie's safety, and maybe Sophie can learn to help you feed the cows and horse. Everyone will have to learn new skills and help out wherever they can. I know it's going to be hard, but we really need everyone's help now. They'll be plenty of time to play on other days."

"One thing is different here, though." Rob's voice grew serious. "When we lived in the old house, we kept Sunday just for the Lord, but here the work still has to be done. After morning chores are done, we'll harness the horse and take the wagon to Grandpa's and go to church with him, but Mama will stay here with Sophie. However, sometimes there will be important work that will need to be done and it can't be put off. A farm is a little different from a house in the city. Remember, Sunday is still the Lord's Day, so if we do necessary chores or have to finish some work, we'll do it to his honor."

Kristine, who had been listening intently to Rob's dictums, hurried to the table as her husband concluded his lecture.

"There's one last thing. When school begins in late summer, everyone will attend, every day—and do their chores, too. School is very important and there will be no missed days unless you're really sick. On this your Poppa and I agree, even though there is so much to do."

All of a sudden William swung around in his chair and faced his parents. The young man had been secretly planning his future and it didn't include school. He listened intently to their every word. Could they read his mind, he wondered? They always stayed ahead of his thinking. What could he do now except say what he was on his mind?

"Poppa, I know how busy you'll be, don't you think I should be helping you here on the farm or at your work?" he blurted out. "Lots of boys my age are working full time. Going to school isn't that important right now."

"William, we'll have no more of that talk," Rob said. "The matter is closed. You will stay in school. An education is what you need for the future. There are many lads with a strong back but few with a strong mind."

Ugh! William thought to himself. *I hate school and now I have to go to church too. Nothing has changed.* William couldn't see it yet, but much was changing.

"Kristine is there one more cup of coffee? I just need to sit a little longer and think about everything that's happened today." The hot coffee was comforting and relaxing. Rob's mind quickly wandered to his most unsettling thoughts.

Yes I have strong attitudes about work, church, and play and they're the foundation of everything I believe in, but every day this new life we've chosen is forcing me to rethink what I've taken for granted all my life. My children are changing. They're growing taller and stronger, but they're growing in other ways too, in their independence, self-confidence, skills, and attitudes. I admire Kristine's ability to adapt to these changes but it's not so easy for me. Sophie is changing too. It's hard for me to just let her go, to experience life and learn on her own. I want to pull her back, to protect her from harm, but she's so independent, so wants to be her own person. She's trying to help, to contribute to the family. Now she can even feed herself some easy-to-eat foods, which is a great help to Kristine. When we lived in the city, life had become such a challenge for her but now she's enjoying a freedom she never could have known in our old home. I really believe that in the end this move will prove that it was worth all our struggles, even though right now, life is hard for everybody.

I remember when I was a young boy; I thought my father was unreasonable, too, but in the end I have to believe that my father's ideas were best. Kristine said that there is always friction, a kind of pull and tug between parents and their children, but my father's rules and decisions were based on his beliefs and so are mine. That is the way it is in life. There are rules to follow. But, if I were honest with myself it would have been wonderful if some of those decisions could have been mine and not his.

We Plow The Fields And Scatter The Good Seed On The Land...

"Rob, have you decided where the garden will go? If this family is going to have food next winter, that garden must be started. We've been here almost two months and not one spade of soil has been turned."

Next to drawing plans for houses, plants were one of Rob's true loves. Every year, even in the city, he'd always planted a small backyard garden. Other families did the same, but for Rob, gardening gave him a sense of peace. He would always remark that when he put his hands into the soil and nurtured those tiny plants to life, he felt close to his creator—a feeling that brought him inner joy.

"Kristine, you know how busy we've all been. I just haven't had time to start that project. One project at a time, that's all I can do." But today he could see that Kristine was going to push the issue and he guessed that she would have her way.

"Well Rob, the sun is shining this morning. Let's go outside and find the best spot right now."

"Right now? I have to do some planning first, and besides, I haven't finished my morning coffee." Rob planned out every project in detail, but Kristine just dove in feet first.

"Yes, right now." Kristine reached over and took the coffee cup right out of Rob's hand. "When we settle on a garden plot, I'll refill the cup with fresh."

Rob had been challenged.

Finding a good garden plot proved easy. Across the yard there was a space that was little more than an old plot of pasture separated from the house by a beautiful stonewall. On the house side of the wall, an abandoned road severed the would-be lawn into two parts, but on this June morning little green could be found in either section. Rob and Kristine began to explore the land on the field side of the wall.

"Someone had a garden here not that long ago," Rob dug his heel into the soil and kicked the winter rubble away. "Looks like good soil, and this spot has a southern exposure. Feel the warmth on these rocks, Kristine. The wall will capture the sun's heat in the spring and protect our plants from the northwest wind. Yes, this should be our spot."

Rob continued examining the space. "Been at least two years since this garden was planted, but there's a rhubarb bed that has plants we can use this year. The land that's been used is too small for our garden, but it will be a start."

"Let's pace off the bigger garden right now, Rob. I brought some twine from the house we could use for marking." Using whatever was handy for holding the twine taut, the couple quickly paced off an expanded space and Rob began penciling notes in the little book he always carried.

"We need to have the chickens closer to the garden, so let's move that old hen house in the barnyard over here." Rob was already looking at the project with his architect's eyes. Kristine watched as he drew a little map of the barnyard and garden in his book, marking not only the hen house, but also where the sun would fall and what part of the garden would be shaded by the ancient yard trees during the day. "Got to make a plan; each type of vegetable has a perfect place for growing. Now all we have to do is turn this soil over, add some manure, and plant a garden." Kristine sighed; sometimes Rob simplified very difficult tasks.

* * * * * * * *

The garden was to be a family affair, just like everything else. When the family lived in the city, Rob and Kristine's purpose had been to give Sophie a safe life and to keep William from destroying himself, but now they had two additional tasks: keep a dry roof over their heads and put food on the table.

"Children," Kristine announced at breakfast. "Today Poppa and I will need everyone's help in the garden. Willi, I think even Sophie can help if you work with her."

"Oh no!"

"Ugh!"

"Mama, do we have to?" A chorus of groans and resistance arose only to be met eyeball to eyeball with Mama's steely glare. The children knew they had lost this battle and begrudging followed their father to the garden spot that now was simply an early spring hayfield. Rob outfitted each child with appropriate tools, shovels, spades, picks, and buckets.

"Here's our plan," he announced. "William and I will loosen the sod in large clumps, Mama will pull the sod apart with this hook so it's loose enough to pull free. Then everyone else will pick up the sod and carry it to a pile outside the garden."

The old garden space was easily reclaimed, but the new garden space was different. The years-old hay field valiantly fought back against the family—it wanted to stay hayfield. The shovels and spades dug, the picks loosened soil, but the hayfield had been there so long that the roots of the tall grasses clutched other roots and all entwined to make an impenetrable mass. After hours of toil and little progress, almost everyone had had enough.

"Poppa, my hands hurt. Look at my fingers. I think these welts are going to burst. I'll bleed to death if I turn one more shovel of sod." Beth, slightly prone to the melodramatic, cried the lament felt by everyone.

"Rob, I really don't believe we can hand dig the rest of this garden. We need to stop now, before someone gets hurt. You're soaking wet from this backbreaking work. Honestly, it looks like you've been out in a rainstorm. Maybe the Chamberlains owned a plow that the horse could pull and break up this stubborn sod. The children could start a treasure hunt to see if they can find one. Anyway, right now everyone needs to eat something and rest for a bit."

"Kristine, you are always our voice of reason. Lunch break, everyone."

****

The next morning, the family gathered in the to-be-garden space.

"Wow, Buster looks handsome in that work harness," Beth exclaimed. "I hope he knows what to do."

William, who had learned to work with the horses when he helped out at the lumberyard, positioned the horse into place and securely fastened the harness to the sod-breaking plow that the children had uncovered in a corner of the barn's basement.

"Now children, everyone stay back with your Mama while we see how this goes. William, I'll handle the plow and you drive Buster. Let's give this a try."

What a challenge. Neither William nor Rob had ever plowed using a horse, but Buster had plowed many furrows. A bit lazy from years of inactivity, the horse initially resisted the work, balking when the plow blade dug into the earth. Rob and William coaxed the horse forward, and reluctantly he began to pull.

At first Rob tried handling the plow, but William proved better suited for this task as the young man had grown tall and possessed the strength of youth. They quickly found that rather than trying to drive Buster through the garden, the horse preferred to have Willi lead him down each furrow. The plow's curved steel dug into the brown soil, exposing both rich soil and a bountiful crop of New England rocks. Kristine and the children, each carrying a small bucket, fanned out behind the plow, picking the ancient glacial chards from the soil.

"Willi, let Poppa lead Buster for a while. I need you to help Sophie. Show her how to pick the rocks and put them in the bucket. Beth, put that full bucket over there at the corner of the garden and then help Dottie. Her bucket is too heavy." Kristine spent more time directing the children than picking rocks, but for everyone, the work was backbreaking and exhausting.

It took a full day to plow the plot, another day to fertilize the garden with manure hauled from the manure pile, and then one last day with an ancient horse-drawn cultivator to make the garden ready. The once used garden space had workable soil and would support plants this year, but the new space cut from virgin hayfield would take a full growing year with a crop to break the sod up properly. Rob had planned to send away for seeds and plants, but they were running out of time to establish their garden, so the problem of the moment became where could they get seeds to plant? Mama had brought some sprouting potatoes from the city, but that would not be enough.

Spring Planting

"There must be some vegetable seeds here somewhere! Everyone kept seeds for the next year." Mama explained to the children. "I need you to hunt through the barn and I'll go through the cellar. Poppa's records said that he bought seed corn for planting with the farm."

But try as they might, the family found only a handful of corn seed. The mice, rats and squirrels had had a very good winter.

Next year the family would send away to a big seed house for good fresh seed, but this year they would have to buy seed locally. Now that the garden plot was finished, Poppa turned to planning this year's garden in detail. That night as he leafed through some seed catalogues he had an idea about what to do with their first year garden space, but he wasn't going to say anything until he had more information.

As soon as breakfast was finished Rob made an announcement. "Kristine, I need to go into town. I'll be gone most of the morning."

Kristine watched him hitch Buster to the wagon and drive from the yard. *Strange,* she said to herself, *he didn't even ask me if I needed anything for the house. He must be on a mission.*

****

"Morning Mr. Johnson. No Marten this morning?"

Rob's father had been quick to introduce Rob to all the merchants and farm suppliers he wanted his son to use. "Rob," he'd told his son, "there are honest and dishonest men in this world. The good Lord has blessed the men I'll introduce you to with ethics, fair pricing and a love for the Good Lord. It would be wise to keep them in business." For most of his "shopping" trips Marten oversaw his son's purchases. It gave Rob a built-in voucher for extending credit, as each merchant knew Marten would guarantee the deal. Marten liked being in control.

"Nope. Here by myself this morning, and I've an odd question for you. I'm hoping you have some type of seed corn that not too expensive. I need to break up my new garden plot and planting corn would do it. I'd like it to be edible too, not cattle feed."

"Well," the proprietor said, "I guess you came to the right place. Just got a sack of special ordered premium sweet corn seed for a local farmer. He refused the order cause the sack was ripped and the seeds had scattered all over my storeroom. Now, I can't sell it at a profit. I just haven't had the time to clean up the spilled seeds and by the end of the week the rats and squirrels will have taken all that great corn. What a shame. If you want to clean up that mess for me, you can have what corn is left for a real bargain price. We both win, you get some great corn and I get that mess cleaned up."

Rob couldn't wait to tell his tale and burst into the kitchen just before the evening meal. "Kristine, wait till you see what I've got! Premium sweet corn seed, about the best one can buy and what a bargain I got it for." Rob was beside himself as he showed off the pail of seed. "I've got enough seed to plant most of the new garden space in sweet corn. We'll have corn to eat, probably have enough for you to can, and maybe we can trade some for vegetables we won't be growing this year."

* * * * * * * * *

Getting a job that paid real wages was hard to find, but because Rob and William were Swedes and Swedes had a good reputation in town for honest work well done, the pair was able to get some honest work for real money. With some of that money, Rob returned to the farm store and purchased more seeds, some vegetables that were already growing in little pots, and more seed potatoes. Their garden would be late, but hopefully it would be a long growing season.

One day in late summer, William surprised everyone. "Mama, close your eyes, no peeking either." With that he pulled the husk back on a tender ear of sweet corn and positioned it right under her nose. "Okay, what did I find?"

"Oh, William! Sweet corn, we have fresh sweet corn. Let's go right now and pick enough ears for our supper." The family was thrilled.

"Mama," Beth said after their evening meal. "That corn was so tender and sweet. I never had such a delicious supper. Did you see Sophie's face? She thought it was so funny that everyone was eating with their hands too, not just her. I think she thought we were playing a game with her. I can't wait to have sweet corn again."

Rob had been working a small job at a YMCA camp not too far from town and he just happened to tell his co-workers that their family had extraordinary sweet corn for supper the night before. The story spread like wild fire, so it was no accident that when Kristine answered a knock at their door later that morning, she found a stranger looking for sweet corn.

"Morning Mrs. Johnson. I'm from the Y camp and I hear you have sweet corn. Will you sell the camp some? We'll pay you real money for the food and if it's as good as your husband says, we'll want some more tomorrow."

Mama couldn't believe what she was hearing. She and the children went to the garden and filled a bushel basket. The folding money went into the crock atop the tall kitchen cabinet. It was Kristine's savings bank, a special place where meager extra coins were kept, but now the corn money had begun to fill it like never before.

The children begged for more sweet corn dinners, but they had had their first and last meal of sweet corn. Every day for the entire corn-growing season, the camp bought all the corn the family could grow and harvest. When the last ear had been picked, the last corn stalk turned into feed for the cows and horse, Rob sat back with his cigar and realized what a blessing the sweet corn seed had been for them.

Their first summer had been successful beyond belief. Winter would be here soon, but the house was habitable and Kristine had canned many of the extra vegetables from their garden. She and the children had cleared out the basement root cellar and stocked it with potatoes, turnips, carrots, beets, and even some gnarly apples gathered from old fruit-bearing trees on the property. Their small herd of animals was now healthy and productive. In addition to the corn stalks, the family had cut and taken in enough hay to feed the animals through the winter. Most importantly, they would be going into the winter with some real money in Mama's special money crock. Nothing could go wrong now.

Winter

All in all, summer had been good to the Johnsons, but the days shortened and the standing water in the watering troughs began to ice over every morning. The early messengers of winter were knocking at their door, and soon the family would discover that this first winter in the country would require them to stretch their skills even further.

The first hint of this came when John and Selma Harris, their closest neighbors, decided to pay a "working" visit. Kristine had not met their neighbors before, but Rob had talked to this tall lanky farmer with a substantial beard growth once or twice across the fence line. He introduced himself when Mama opened to his loud rapping knock.

"John Harris, and this here is my wife Selma. She wanted to meet the new neighbors. I reckon you're Mrs. Johnson." He paused then continued without waiting for an answer. "Your husband around? Have some business to discuss with him."

"Yes, come in. You and your wife live up the hillside, I believe? My pleasure," she said, hesitantly extending her dusty whitened hand. "Excuse the flour, been making bread. The first batch is about perfect to eat now so I hope you'll have some with a cup of coffee. Sit down and I'll send one of the girls to get Rob, he and William are down in the pasture mending a broken fence."

It took a while for Rob to make his way back to the house. "John Harris, hello neighbor. What brings you down the hill on this early winter's day? Actually I was a bit glad when Beth said we had company. I'm sweaty and dirty, but glad to take a rest right about now."

Pleasantries out of the way, John Harris began. "Rob, don't know if you know about the ice agreement Ol' Charlie Chamberlain and I had. Probably no one told you, but that pond across the road from your land, well, it's been an ice pond for your farm and mine for more years then either of us has been alive. That's why you folks have an ice house."

Rob leaned forward. "An ice house! Where?"

"Back of your barn, that little poke-out with the double walls. Charlie and I tightened it up real good four or five years ago. Year before last the ice lasted until fourth of July, but not the year he died, that was a bad year for ice and Charlie."

"Anyway, in good times we'd share the job of cutting the ice from my pond, haul it up here to your ice house and tote sawdust up here from the nearest mill. Provides ice for you and me all winter. Don't know what you're doing for cooling food right now, but the ice box is still the best."

They did have an icebox, but in the city the iceman had come by with huge blocks and they lasted long enough to keep everything safe and healthy until he returned. Ice was not too hard to come by in the city, but out here there was no iceman, so they had made waterproof containers and lowered the most perishable food down the well, where everything stayed cool and safe. If there was a special occasion, Rob would buy a huge block of ice in town and carry it home in the wagon. The ice would be wrapped in multiple layers of burlap and all the drips caught in a huge pan. Having fresh ice appealed to Mama but even more, she liked the idea of having a supply of ice right here on their own farm.

"Well Johnson, here's my idea: You've got a son that can supply some labor at loading and packing the ice. I've got a team of horses and most of the ice tools. If the winter is cold, we might get four or five cuttings."

Rob leaned forward again. "So John, tell me how it works, the cutting, that is."

Harris began to describe the process in detail. "When the pond is frozen enough to hold our weight—usually almost a foot thick—we venture out onto it and use large saws and cut the ice into chunks; I've got a huge clamp that attaches to the ice and we let the horse pull the block out of the pond, then use ice tongs to load it onto a wagon or sleigh and haul it up to the ice house. There we pack it in sawdust and shavings from the sawmill and cover it with layers of burlap. Ice will last till late summer if we're lucky. Most of the work is hard, but your girls can help by covering the ice with the sawdust and burlap."

Rob smiled. Hard work, he realized, but cool drinks and maybe ice cream in August… now that would be a real treat. "Okay, John. Now you have a new deal."

That winter, the Johnson's learned the hard way how to have safe food and cool drinks. That year the last hard freeze came about the middle of February, but by then the last of the ice had been cut, hauled and stacked. The icehouse was tightly packed with giant ice chunks, sawdust, and burlap.

* * * * * *

Once the cold set in for their first winter, the kerosene kitchen range wasn't enough to comfortably heat the house.

"Rob," Kristine said one morning. "Do you think any of the fireplaces are workable? I know one is blocked by the kitchen range, but there are two more and maybe a third. If one of them worked, maybe we could have some heat in the living room, especially on Sundays? I know your plans are to get another kerosene space heater, but we don't have that yet and there's lots of scrap wood here, enough to burn for a while."

Rob looked at his wife and shifted his weight from one foot to the other. She could tell he was uncomfortable. "Don't know, Kristine. Haven't had a chance to inspect those chimneys and you know the girls get scared when we light fires. Remember how scared Sophie got when we burned the brush in the lower pasture?" But he did have to admit that the house was cold and he hadn't saved enough to buy a space heater yet. "Tell you what, I'll take a good look at the fireplaces and chimneys right now.

After about an hour's work Rob came to some conclusions. "I think if we do a good cleaning on the living room chimney it might work. It does look like it hasn't been used in a while. Let me get William to help; I need someone on the roof and someone down here in the living room."

William climbed up on the roof carrying a bag of straw and two long ropes. He threw one rope down the chimney and tied his end to the bag of straw, then tied the other rope to the opposite end of the bag of straw.

"Poppa, pull on the line," William called down to his father. Rob pulled the bag down and then William drew the bag of straw up. Up and down the small bag of straw was drawn through the chimney until old soot and bird's nests cluttered the hearth.

"After we clean up this mess," Rob said to the band of curious children, "we'll try a small fire and see how it draws."

Rob laid a tiny fire and set it ablaze. The dry tinder caught quickly.

"No smoke in the house, chimney has a good draw," he said to Kristine. "Let's put a few more sticks on and let it burn a bit." The fire quickly warmed the room.

"Oh, this feels so good," Kristine exclaimed. "I can see us all sitting here around this cheery fire telling stories and then falling asleep."

"Poppa," little Dottie said excitedly. "Look up there! The chimney is blowing smoke rings just like you do with your cigar. See, right up there on the side of the chimney." The little girl pointed to a place near the ceiling where a trail of puffy white smoke was leaking out between the over-dry ancient bricks.

Within moments, the tinder-dry horsehair mortar that had held the bricks for decades caught fire and began burning inside the chimney. A foreboding sound began to build within the ancient stack until a frightening roar filled the room. Within minutes the family was fighting a chimney fire.

Kristine beat the hearth fire down while calling to the children, "Get outside, everybody outside, now! Willi, take care of Sophie. Go to the barn, everyone, now!"

The children, having immediately realized the chimney was burning, ran for the door. Panic had seized them even before the first words had left Mama's mouth. Fire was not their friend.

Rob tried to block the flue and cut off the draft from the fireplace side while William bounded to the rooftop again and stuffed the chimney top with burlap bags. Cutting off the airflow was working, but not entirely.

Rob filled buckets from the livestock's watering trough. "William, pour water down on the flames. I'll keep it coming. Beth, pump more water."

The fire sputtered, billowed steam and white smoke, and then died. Luckily, the family had controlled the fire before it had broken through the chimney wall.

"Oh, this place smells horrible," Beth remarked as she timidly re-entered the house. Sooty black water, burned wood, and crumbling chimney covered the living room floor and a dark black film now clung to the plaster ceiling.

One step forward, two steps back, Mama thought. *But thank the Lord, the house is still standing, we are alive and all right, just scared and jittery.*

The next morning Kristine took the money jar down from atop the kitchen cabinet.

"Rob, the corn money was meant for something special or an emergency. Count out the cost of a kerosene space heater, I really think there's enough there."

During the next two weeks, three things happened. First every fireplace was covered up and blocked off, then the kerosene space heater arrived, and finally, winter set in with a vengeance.

Willi's Story

(Willi recalls Sophie and her adjustment to living in the country)

When we first moved to the farm, I missed my city life so much. I missed playing with my friends, the glass pile, and our neighborhood games of marbles. Mama said young ladies didn't play marbles, but I did what I wanted, even if it wasn't ladylike. I even missed Jonnie, the neighborhood bully, but I'll always remember him with pride for the huge scar I bore on my chin. For me, the move was hard. It frightened me—so many new things, so much I didn't understand. I liked it where life had been predictable.

The day we moved, I lost my most precious possession, my pencil box. In that little wooden box were my treasures. There were my game pieces from the glass pile; some coins, including a fifty-cent piece my neighbor gave me for helping her; and my pencils, all colorful and sharp. My eight-year old life was in that box. I had put the little box on the back shelf of Mr. Rawson's car and during the trip the box fell between the seat and the frame of the car. The trip had been so hard on Mama. She was unusually grumpy and sharp tongued. Sophie's wiggling, squirming and fidgeting didn't help matters one bit either. Mr. Rawson kept losing his temper, and boy did he have a temper, so asking someone to pull the car apart for my pencil box was just out of the question. I counted it gone.

After Uncle Nat brought the animals back to Poppa's farm, I forgot all about the pencil box. I was in heaven. William was my partner and I helped him with the animals. He taught me everything and after I learned to do my jobs, he let me take over his jobs, too. Poppa was angry every time that happened, but I didn't need his blessing. Besides, I always had something to hold over William when I really needed a favor. I learned to milk the cow, lead the horse, and even ride him bareback. Of course we didn't have a saddle, but bareback was fine. During the next couple of years I learned to drive Buster when he was harnessed to the carriage, but Poppa said that if I drove the buggy someone older had to be there just in case.

I just loved everything about the farm and even though I was in charge of Sophie, she loved the animals and learned to follow me around and help too, so we both won. Beth would get angry with me. She'd complain to Mama that I didn't do enough of the housework, but Mama would just say that I was helping out in different ways, and she seemed happy with the arrangement. I did tell Mama that it was hard to do the farm work in a dress and why couldn't I have pants like William even though girls seldom wore pants. But Mama didn't always follow everyone else's thinking, so she took an old pair of William's and cut them down to fit me. I wore them every day until she had to make me a new pair. One thing about Mama, she could sew anything. She made grain sacks or old clothes into the most wonderful garments, some just useful but others were beautiful and stylish.

Even before taking care of the animals, Sophie was my most important charge. She was in my care most of the day except at meals when Mama fed her the foods she couldn't eat by herself. Sophie loved the farm. She'd run and play and had plenty of room around her, as she hated being confined and controlled. Mama had told me about a school she visited with Mrs. Robbson on one of their trips to Europe, I think it was in Switzerland. It was a school where children with difficulties, some like Sophie, lived where they could spend most of their time outside in the country, freely involved in all of life. Mama thought this unrestrained life was what Sophie needed, so most of the time I just had to keep my eye's open to see that she kept out of danger and participated in everything, but Sophie did have some curious habits.

One day, Mama sat all of us down. "Children," she began, "I need you to be truthful in answering this question. I am losing so many plates and cups. Perhaps you are taking them to the barn to feed the animals or outside and have forgotten to bring them back, but I need these in the kitchen. So far I have lost two cups, a dinner plate, two saucers and then just yesterday the gravy boat from my china service disappeared. What is going on?"

I could tell Mama was frustrated but we all swore that we had nothing to do with the mystery of the disappearing dinnerware. I decided, right there and then to solve this mystery. I watched everybody but no one took dishes except one of us, Sophie. That was it! Sophie was the culprit. I watched one day as she slipped a dish off the table when

Mama wasn't looking and snuck it outside. I followed to see what happened. Everyone loves a mystery.

Sophie loved to hoard bright shiny things, and dishes fit the bill, but then what she did next surprised me and everyone else when I told them the story. Sophie would carry her stolen dish to a special "breaking rock" and smash them into pieces. Now she had a puzzle. For days she'd sit there and piece together the chards of the dish, fitting this piece here and that piece there. When she tired of that puzzle, she'd steal another dish and begin the routine again. Mama quickly put all her breakable dishes high on the shelves and only the old already chipped or unusable pieces were left for Sophie to "find."

When she wasn't creating puzzles, Sophie was escorting old shoes everywhere. There were dozens of old shoes discarded around the farm.... seems someone who lived here before us had been employed in the local shoe industry. A worker would drop off shoe parts to the owners who would then put the shoes together. The worker would collect the finished shoes and drop off more parts. Sophie found every shoe part, partially finished or fully completed shoes, and adopted these orphans as her own. For most of her life she could be found carrying one of her children with her, always well protected.

Sophie still had convulsions and seizures, but by now the family took them in stride and everyone knew how to help her if they discovered her in an out of control situation. Doctor's visits had long ceased and her condition simply appeared to be managed. I think Mama and Poppa had just had enough of medicine. There were doctors here, but they only came to the house if someone was really sick.

Mostly Sophie was my charge. I took her with me, played with her and just kept my eye on her. One day something dreadful happened while I was in charge. Sophie, sitting in a pool of warm sunlight that flowed across the open barn floor, was deeply involved in one of her many made up games. The huge rolling door was open and I had led Buster to the rear of the barn, tying him securely, I thought. Anyway, somehow he got loose and something spooked him on his blind side. He turned and raced for the open door with Sophie calmly sitting there right in his path and on his blind side. I knew I couldn't stop the runaway and suddenly visions of Buster trampling my sister to death filled my mind. I froze, unable to move. It was like slow motion, the little girl in the sunlight calmly playing, the giant horse thundering towards her blind to what was ahead of him. She just sat there, never saw him coming, then at the last minute he sensed she was there and leapt over her. I had never seen him jump, not even in the pasture, but that day he jumped in one magnificent leap sailing over my sister leaving her unharmed. She looked up at the horse as he cleared her body, her first awareness that something tragic had just been avoided. I ran over to Sophie, put my arms around her and hugged her until she squealed and I stopped shaking.

Usually Sophie didn't like to be touched or held but for some unknown reason, today she wanted me to hold her. Maybe she sensed what disaster had almost happened. Right then and there I thanked God for protecting both of us. Probably out of fear, I vowed to keep what happened that day a secret and never told anyone. Only when I was much, much older and perhaps wiser did I dare tell the story about how that day unfolded.

The Red Parlor

William finally got his way. It was true, the family needed a truck and so after struggling for too many years with just horsepower, an aging farm truck became the property of the Johnson family. It wasn't pretty, but it worked. If the family wanted to go somewhere together, Kristine would climb in front with Sophie on her lap and Rob and the children piled into the bed. William, the Captain of Transportation, drove.

After one of those Sunday afternoon family visiting days, William rolled the truck to its final stop. Anxious to be free, the children scattered to the furthest reaches of the farm like a flock of birds that flies up and away when scared by a sudden noise. Even Rob quickly entered the house, anxious to change into more comfortable clothes as he had had enough of Sunday visiting. Kristine however, moved slowly, as if a hand was holding her body back. Ever so slowly she moved from the cab of the truck to the house, to her kitchen and then to the parlor, the finest room of the house. She moved toward the most comfortable chair, collapsing into its folds: hat, coat and all, and nobody noticed.

There is a time when we all confront our personal devils, our inner voices, a time of secret questioning. Sometimes we slay those dragons and sometimes they slay us. The family had spent the afternoon visiting their Swedish neighbors, friends who like so many others from their old city had now moved to this region. Kristine, who had enjoyed the afternoon, suddenly found an odd feeling creeping across her mind. The unsettled feeling grew and suddenly engulfed her as if a dark cloud had moved across the sun.

Enfolded within the arms of the soft chair, she indulged in a rare moment of self-pity. She looked about and momentarily closed her eyes. This isn't how she had wanted things. The Carlson's home was so beautiful, the furniture so perfect, the food so delightful, the decorating so New York.

Kristine opened her eyes and looked around the darkening room. She focused her attention on a small, framed photo that sat on a side table next to the Tiffany lamp she'd brought from their city home. The photo, taken in their Hunt Street parlor, was of her, Rob and their first-born son, William. That room had been her pride and joy and she called it her Red Parlor. That room had been her moment of triumph, her pinnacle of personal success. It embodied the finest of the things of life; it echoed the rich interiors of New York, its society's glamour, and her pride at having been a trusted member of a different world. The wall hangings, the beautiful glassware, the elegant oil paintings in bright gilded frames, the richly embossed wall covering and the deep piled oriental carpets; everything had worked so well together. In that room she was a success, a true lady.

When her eyes closed, the parlor still existed. She could mentally walk through the room touching each fringe, chair, or curio. She could lay flat the linens or wish away a spot of dust.

The tears swelled behind her eyes and in a forbidden moment the past and present met, then collided. A lump caught in her throat and a wave of dark washed across her mind. The tears moved forward, wetting her eyes and blurring the sight about her.

A voice from the hallway startled her, "Kristine, where are you?" Rob, with Sophie in tow, entered the parlor but the dimming light of the day almost clothed Mama in obscurity. "Kristine what's the matter? Are you all right? The sun is low; we've got to get the chores done, everyone will want to eat before long and Sophie needs you. Are you sure you're all right?"

Kristine gathered herself, inside and out and simply said as she rose from the chair, "You know Rob, John and Anna Carlson have made their home so lovely." But Poppa was almost beyond earshot, anxious to make up for the time lost on the extra long Sunday visit; Kristine's words lingered only for the walls and the framed photo to hear.

Sophie reached out for Mama's hand and pulled her towards the kitchen, but instead of following the child, Kristine drew Sophie towards her and just held her. No words were needed. It was just one moment, one moment when Sophie didn't resist or pull back from that human embrace. Then the child giggled and playfully hid herself inside Mama's open coat. Richness, Kristine suddenly realized, is measured in many different ways, but today it was hard to embrace the obvious.

Rob's Story

(Rob recalls how he coped with some important challenges)

I had many pleasures in my life, but one that I thoroughly enjoyed was my Sunday afternoons. I guess you'd say I was a man of strong habits, for Sunday afternoon was the only time I allowed myself the leisure of relaxing. The southern side of our home was washed with abundant sunshine, but old colonial homes like ours never had enough windows to let that sunshine into the house. Kristine and I fixed that by ripping out one entire end of a room on the south side and installing windows and a door. The windows bumped out, like a bay window, but they were much bigger, a bit revolutionary for the time. It was a delightful space. Kristine put plants in the sunshine and comfortable chairs nearby.

I especially loved that room. I'd sit and smoke a cigar, another pleasure I allowed myself, and read. I owned some wonderful books: famous sermons and Bible studies. That's how I kept my love of the scriptures alive. Those books had been so important to me when I taught church school in the city, but now I just enjoyed the books for myself and told my versions of Bible stories to the children.

I'd never tell anyone that moving from the city to the country had been easy. I knew it would take a toll on the family, but at the time it seemed the only thing that was reasonable to do. I really believed that the Lord would guide us and help us, but I didn't realize how much he'd leave to us to figure out.

Kristine and I grew closer to each other as we labored together to make our lives and home successful. That was such a blessing. We'd always been special friends, but now there was a bond that was different, better and deeper. That bond helped us as we struggled through those earliest years in the country. We spent more time just talking about how to make things work, what we could afford and what were priorities, but when it came to those things, we had one major problem—my father.

Marten always had very strong opinions and he believed he knew best about how to solve our problems. He had been very supportive, and for that I was thankful, but Kristine and I wanted to make our own decisions about what was needed and what could wait 'til another day. Marten however, would tell us what we needed and almost never took no for an answer.

I remember soon after electricity had been run along the newly improved main road and could be made available to our house, my father told us it was time to put in an indoor bathroom. Our house in the city had had all the modern conveniences of the day and I knew Kristine and the children missed them. It was unpleasant having to use the outhouse in the barn or bedpans at night. Kristine and I sat down and figured that if my work continued we could buy some porcelain fixtures and an electric water pump in about three months and by cold weather I'd have been able to do the carpentry and it would be done all without debt. However, my father had a different idea. Within days, the pump and porcelain fixtures arrived at our home and with it a bill, in this case from Sears Roebuck and Co. marked paid. However, there was a second bill for the exact same amount made out to Marten Johansson with the words, "put on the account of Rob Johnson." A partial payment was expected each month. I'd get so mad, but Marten wasn't one you could reason with. He always had to have things his way. Thank the Lord for Kristine; she was so good at keeping me from exploding in some angry manner. It wasn't easy, but somehow I got that devil under control. Things did seem to work out between Marten and myself, but most of that was thanks to Kristine.

It didn't take long for friends and relatives to find their way to our part of the country. Some came to visit, especially during the hot summer months, while others came to visit and then bought homes and made their lives here. That's one thing about living in the city, the summers were always too hot and the stagnant air smelled of rotting garbage. Out here, the air was sweet smelling and the occasional heat wave bearable.

The relatives and friends came in droves; they helped us to be sure. More hands to help bring in the hay; to contribute labor to our endless list of building projects; and to provide companionship for Kristine, who sometimes got lonely for news from the city. But eventually, the price of having so much company began to take its toll.

There were too many mouths to feed and there was never enough food to go around. Finally, Kristine put her foot down.

"If you come, you must bring food," she told everyone—and of course they still came, but now they all brought groceries and baked goods, too. The children were happy to give up their rooms to the guests as it meant they got to sleep in the soft hay of the barn, just as they had years earlier when we first moved to the country.

I loved gardening; I hadn't realized how much until we were at it for several years. It took work, but everyone pitched in. One day, while I was working for a family in town they approached me about their orchard. Seems they had recently planted an apple and fruit orchard and now they wanted to do something different with the land. They told me I could have all the fruit trees, about two-dozen or so. All we had to do was dig up the young trees and replant them. Honestly, that would be a challenge, but what an offer! It was too good to pass up.

The entire family plus the old truck descended upon the orchard and we dug and dug and dug. We wrapped the tree roots in wet burlap and carted them home only to dig more holes here and replant the trees. It took hours of backbreaking work, but eventually—after several years—we had an orchard that bore cherries, pears, and apples. Now that we had fruit trees, I was prompted to learn beekeeping and soon we were harvesting honey while the bees pollinated the fruit.

I kept expanding the garden. Most crops I grew were prolific and abundant but I was especially proud when my melons and strawberries won awards at the county fair for being the best grown in the region. I also grew grapes, three types to be exact. One variety made a fine homemade drink that Kristine swore wasn't alcoholic, but sometimes I wondered if she was telling the truth. She told me it was an old recipe from Sweden, but for some reason she never let me watch her make the mixture to be bottled. On top of the regular cooking and baking, Kristine had her hands full trying to can all that produce, so I put a small addition on the house for a summer kitchen; that made her life much easier.

When we came to the farm, the only trees around were already ancient maples and oaks, but Kristine loved flowers the way I loved vegetables. We hadn't been here too many years before she began one of her famous campaigns: to beautify the grounds of the house. She was relentless. She and the girls planted evergreen trees they dug up in the forest. I sent away for Norway spruce and White Cedar seedlings. We dug flowerbeds and when I was too busy to help, she'd fill pails of dirt and manure and build up the low spots and create islands of beauty. We actually grew grass on a lawn and William or Willi mowed it with a cranky old push mower. Kristine's little spot of heaven was beginning to bloom.

I guess I'd have to say that I changed, too. When we lived in the city all I did was work; work at my job and work at being a church leader. The time I spent with my family, enjoying them as people, the time I spent with Kristine…well, I guess my priorities were different then. I still retained my faith, oh yes, that would never change, but somehow here on our farm, I spent more time trying to practice my faith, rather than trying to preach it. Like my father, I still had strong opinions about things, and one way or another life had to work out the way I wanted it, but somehow the country had changed me. I was a little different, a little easier to get along with… at least most of the time.

I still drew plans for homes, but they were for me to use, not someone else. My architect's office became my woodworking shop. When things got to be too much, I'd retreat to my shop and work with wood in a different way. I loved the smell, the feel of the wood on my hands, and the challenge of creating new things from a solid block of wood. But now, I always left the shop door open. I wanted to include my family, not exclude them.

Life Goes On

With the passage of time, the Johnson household continued to change. A national depression slowly worked its way from the epicenters of urban America to the valleys and byways of its rural cousin. In the city, apples were peddled for pennies, but in the country the sun still shone, the rain fell, and the apples continued to grow. For the Johnsons, there was food on the table and fun to be had around the piano and in the library. So much of what challenged the rest of America had little effect on the family's daily life.

The family had moved beyond survival and both Rob and Kristine began to believe that their deeply held dreams and goals—not only for themselves, but also for each of their children—might be achievable. Like many immigrant families, their greatest desire was that the lives of their children would be easier and better than theirs had been. One of Kristine's deeply held goals was that her daughters would go to college and graduate. The money jar atop the kitchen cabinet now held money towards that goal, but with the newspapers reporting rumbles of a national financial crisis, some goals now seemed less attainable than others.

"Kristine, we need to talk about William," Rob said one evening after everyone had gone to bed. "He asked me if he could be honest with me. Of course I said yes, and then he began what ended up being a really good talk. He told me he appreciates that we enrolled him in the trade school he's been attending, but he says he's just not a student. Learning a trade is a good idea, but not the way he's doing it now. He's got some ideas for his own business and he wants our support and the chance to let him try."

Kristine wasn't surprised at the turn of events. She'd recently gotten a letter from her sister in Sweden and learned that Emma's boys were now dairymen. Kristine had told William about the letter and he'd questioned her at great length about what Emma's boys did for a living and how the system worked in Sweden. She guessed that his business idea had something to do with that letter.

"William isn't going to stay in school," Rob said. "For the time being, I have plenty of work for him and I'll pay him the same as the other men, but if he develops this idea, I'll give him the time to try and make it work. I even told him he could use the farm truck if he needed it to get started."

Kristine knew Rob was right. "Time to let the young man try what is in his heart," she said.

Using the family's old farm truck, William established a small egg and milk business. He'd drive to the local farms, collect their milk and eggs, and then transport them to a dairy where the commodities were sold, and then he'd pay the farmers for their milk and produce and take a fee for being the middleman. The only thing they asked of William in return for using the old truck was that he contributed some money to the college fund jar atop the kitchen cabinet.

Beth's Story
(Beth recalls how Sophie's maturing caused problems)

We all began to worry about Mama after her visit to the Carlson's. Suddenly she seemed unhappy much of the time, but that concern began in earnest when she broke her leg. She had been pushing herself so hard, like some inner demon had an agenda for her and she was constantly falling behind. The accident happened one day after a light snow covered the yard. She was hurrying back from the chicken coop and stepped on an icy patch; down she went. The doctor said her leg was badly broken, so he bound it up till it mended, but that didn't stop her. She took a straight-backed kitchen chair and used it like a walker to help her get around, and just kept going.

At the time, I was in high school and studying to be a secretary, so I often helped Mama write letters to her sister Emma in Sweden. Mama use to write in Swedish but she was losing her Swedish language skills so I wrote in English. Emma had learned to read and write in English when she lived in America, but sometimes the letters were half English and half Swedish. Sometimes Mama still wrote her own letters and occasionally Poppa wrote to Emma's family, but mostly I wrote for them.

Mama worked so hard. She'd stay up 'til late at night sewing clothes for all the family. Her father had been a tailor and she had learned the skills of a seamstress early in her life and never forgot how to use them. She was a wonderful cook, too. One of her early American jobs before she went to work for the Robbsons had been as an assistant cook for another well-to-do family. One night they served dinner to Mark Twain and Mama was so proud of her part in that accomplishment, as the dinner was to be prepared and served in total silence. According to her employer, she and the staff pulled it off perfectly.

Mama never talked much about her life before Poppa. It was always so secretive, something she didn't want to or couldn't talk about.

We'd tease her and try to get her to tell stories, but every time she'd just smile, shoo us out of the kitchen and tell us it "wasn't good fishing weather."

Sophie was maturing and at the same time she was becoming more difficult to control. It was like her body and emotions were being pulled apart. Sometimes nothing would satisfy or calm her. I think the changes scared her and she didn't know what to do. She'd react in her own way and it was tough on all of us, 'cause her reactions were always different.

One day she became very emotional. Her convulsions were different now, more inward directed than physical displays. Anyway, that day she was screaming a lot and being physical with everyone, pushing and shoving us. Then suddenly, she was gone, just gone. We checked everywhere; she was nowhere to be found. Mama was almost hysterical with worry and honestly Willi, Dottie and I shared that anxiety too. Sophie was gone for more than an hour when suddenly Willi spotted her climbing down out of a tree. She had climbed into a tree with a good supply of branches. We children had forgotten that William had laid some boards on those branches and made a platform for us, an open-air tree house. Once we took Sophie up there and she'd remembered how to get there. After that when Sophie needed time alone—and she often did—she'd climb up into the tree and curl up for an hour or two.

Sophie's unpredictability was taking a toll on Mama's health so I took a year off from high school to help Mama with the housework and Sophie. Although we children didn't know it at the time, Mama was beginning to develop heart problems. My extra help at home really benefited her, as she began to get stronger. When I started school again, as Mama flat out insisted that I do, both Willi and I were in the same grade and planned to finish high school the same year. As those last years of high school passed, Mama kept working on her plan. She would not be deterred from success; Willi and I were going to go to college, no matter what.

I don't know how Mama and Poppa managed it, but Willi and I were accepted at a teachers college in Virginia. They worked and saved to pay the bill, but I think Grandpa Marten helped them raise the last of the money they needed for that first year. Mama said we needed to be able to be independent and be able to make it on our own, just in case we didn't get married, which she hoped we'd do someday. It was the time of women's rights and voting, which I always suspected was somehow behind her goals for Willi and myself. One day I asked Mama what she thought of all those ideas. "Right now, Beth, I'll just follow my husband's thinking and let him make the decisions, but I'll be sure my daughters are prepared for the future."

The summer we left for our second year of college, things had become rather stressful. I didn't want to go because Sophie had been sick much of the summer, just one thing after the other. The doctor came to the house several times, but there really wasn't anything wrong, but I thought maybe her body was just wearing out, Mama's certainly was.

September 1931

The long ago deaths of her baby sister and then her mother when she was little more than a child herself had steeled Kristine's heart to sorrow and stolen a sliver of her soul. But now in the stillness of the sickroom, she could not consent to release this child to death's demanding grip. Kristine reached out and stroked the child's cheek; her fingers followed the curved lines of Sophie's delicate features. The child's chin and jaw line, her nose and cheek, they were features she saw in her own face and in the hazy images Kristine's mind carried of her mother's image, visions that still haunted her mind. Sophie's face, it was generational and so deeply personal.

One more time Kristine's hand returned to stroke the child's delicate features. Dare she believe for just one moment that death had been cheated? Her fingers still felt the skin's warmth on her fingertips, but as deeply as she tried to will it so, there was no calling the child back. Sophie could not, nor would not, return to the world of mortals. This child, this special child, now belonged to a band of cherished angels.

Death comes silently, but the absence of life rises like a giant wave of cold and black, roiling and twisting as it forces its presence upon the living. Kristine—the Mama who almost never cried, who always found a way around every obstacle, who never broke—could not stop the sound that tore the very fiber of her soul apart. A wave of torment broke over her and she fell, sobbing, into the bedclothes of the precious little girl who lay still and silent upon the bed. She wept for her daughter, she wept with relief and she wept with the guilt she bore, but she wept too for her lost life.

Rob worked his grief the only way that was possible for him; he made Sophie's coffin. Simple pine boards worked with loving care. He toiled in his workshop, his hiding place, and poured his love and grief into the task. And when it was complete, the simple pine coffin was placed in the finest room of the family home, the big living room.

Each day friends and family called to pay their respects. The visitors, one by one, were ushered into the parlor and with hushed voices offered kind words of condolence, but Kristine sat in stony silence, barely acknowledging the visitors. Perhaps, during those lonely hours beside the child's coffin, she once again traveled the journey they had taken together, a journey that had begun 16 years ago on a September day in 1914; the day the convulsions began. Then, on the afternoon of the third day as the minister uttered words of eternal life in Christ, the child was laid to rest beneath the soil of a Connecticut hillside and Kristine's youngest daughter, son, and husband helped her return to the car and then to their home. Winter had arrived.

Dottie's Story
(Dottie tells about life after Sophie's death)

During most of Sophie's life I was too young to really know what was happening, but by the time Sophie passed away I was in high school and the only daughter left at home with Mama and Poppa. It was left to me to pick up the pieces of my shattered family.

The year before Sophie died I had started high school and my two sisters went off to college. I helped Mama in every way I could, but Sophie was now totally in Mama's care. Poppa and William couldn't help Mama very much as they worked at every job they could get to pay the bills and keep my sisters in school. Mama always put the family ahead of herself and little by little her strength got sucked away and she had a harder and harder time making it through the day.

When I wasn't in school, I worked right along with Mama, learning to cook her recipes, sew garments as beautifully as she did, and generally receiving a massive tutorial in how to run a home and house with as much class as possible in those times of little money. I always remember her saying that one should not be ashamed to wear a patched garment if the patching was done right and neatly.

When we came home from the church the day of Sophie's funeral, Mama was beyond consoling. She went into the bedroom, told everyone to leave her alone, and closed the door. I think she cried herself to sleep every night, 'cause her face was red and puffy each morning. We were worried as she refused food for days and then ate little after that. She had slipped into a deep depression and we couldn't shake her from that state.

Poppa wasn't in much better shape, but at least he could go out and with William do the chores and keep things going, but Mama could do almost nothing. I was so worried… it was as if Mama would bear the guilt of Sophie's condition and death for her entire life, which right now I feared might end soon.

One thing about Sophie's death is that my sisters, Beth and Willi, didn't know Sophie had died. No telegram had been sent to their school, letters were slow, and a telephone call for that distance was unheard of, but the girls had to be told. Mama and Poppa had friends who lived near the school in Virginia, but it was still a two-day drive away. William and I decided that we needed to tell them in person. We sent a telegram and arranged to stay with Mama's friends and set out to visit the school and my sisters. Poppa stayed home and though it was a hard and difficult trip, it was the right thing to do. The trip was the beginning of Mama's healing.

Even while in high school, I loved fashion and style. Eventually that would be my chosen profession, but right then, I just loved to try new hairstyles and create fashions like the ones I saw in magazines. Poppa and I thought that if I trimmed Mama's hair and fashioned it into a new hairstyle she might feel better. Then I spruced up the housedresses she almost always wore by adding some trim and sewing in some form-fitting pleats. You could tell that it made her feel good because when she looked into her mirror a faint sparkle returned to her eyes for a brief moment. What I did made a difference.

It took a long time, but soon Mama began to feel better, to eat again (my cooking was not too bad) and to look healthier. She still had a long journey to walk in her lifetime, and some of it along very dangerous terrain, but I know that in those years after Sophie died I became the family's "Mama," if only for a short time.

What Mama needed now was a new campaign, something to fight for, and that's just what happened. Her new goal was clear, no matter what happened, no matter how bad the economy, I would complete my training to be a hairdresser and the girls would graduate from college. She attacked those goals with renewed vigor, but that is a story for another day.

And Then...

The unmarked graves on the hillside of the local cemetery mark Sophie, Kristine and Rob's final resting place. Farm fields splay out from that resting place and in death their graves lie in land so like the motherland that bore their roots. Long gone are the beautiful plants that once marked those graves, victims of changing rules and efficiency. Now the quiet breezes, the gusts and blows and the daily changing landscape painted by the master artist of the natural world is all that marks their passing. While their bodies rest on that hillside, it is that once run-down farm of yester-year, several miles distant that wormed its way into the very fiber of the entire family's being. If there is a resting place for their souls, then this is where their souls lie, in this place they all called home.

When the winds blow through the tall grasses of the hayfield, you hear their song singing like a heavenly symphony, and when the sun rises beyond the grandfather Maple along the North-South turnpike that still defines the front yard, it is the same vision they saw. When peaches and apples fall to the ground from trees planted by their struggling but hopeful hands, future generations can know that their efforts were not for naught. They left more than a house, a history or values—they left us a vision for living life. Sophie's life was short, it was different, and it challenged the entire family. The family met that challenge and their legacy challenges each of us, even today.

Life is a wind that blows both fair and foul, but blow it will and each of us must find our way.

Epilogue

A Hiding Place From the Wind is based on the life and times of my grandparents, their family, and their home in Northeastern Connecticut. It was this home that inspired the setting for the story and became the *Hiding Place* of the novel. It is a place I know well.

Soon after my husband and I married, we made a monumental decision: we bought the small farm that had been my grandparent's home. Though my grandmother died when I was nine years old, my grandfather lived a long and healthy life. He was able to be a part of my life as I grew into adulthood and lived to attend my college graduation and wedding.

After my grandmother's death, my parents decided it would be easier on everyone if they moved in with my grandfather. This move allowed him to continue to live in his own home and be close to my grandmother's memory. For much of my life, in checkerboard fashion, I have lived under the roof of this *Hiding Place* and do so even today.

When one lives intimately within a space that is so strongly connected to family, the ability to connect to its former inhabitants is intense and constant. I didn't come to this home because it was given to me or because it was the easiest property to buy. No, I came here because the same wind that drove my grandparents to this valley drove my return to this place; I needed to come home.

I have lived within the space that inspired this story. As a child I sat by the fireside and listened to the tales that drove my family's journey. Today I walk the paths my family walked. I touch the totems they touched. It was their past, but it is mine too. Somehow, in ways I will never understand, a certain spirit still resides here. Is the house the same one my grandparents purchased then lived in as a family? No, every timber has been touched and reworked, every board and nail uncovered, every spirit or ghost released to fly, but still the spirit of these people beckoned and called to me.

I have asked myself why I felt driven to write this story. There are many plausible reasons, but perhaps the real reason is not just that the story needed to be told, but that I needed to tell it. When I was born, I came home to the arms of my grandmother, who inspired the Kristine of this story. She was the one who preserved my mother's sanity by holding and rocking this colicky and uncooperative newborn for what must have seemed like an eternity of sleepless nights. During those endless nights while nestled in her arms, I became one in spirit with my grandmother. It's something one feels, a sharing of your souls, and something that has never left me.

But there is more to think about. At three and a half years of age, I contracted polio and was whisked away to a hospital for almost half a year. My parents and grandparents endured months of agony and uncertainty. More importantly, my illness had brought the long dormant fears surrounding my aunt's illness back into sharp focus. My aunt had escaped hospitalization; I had not. She had challenged the family in the harbinger days of WWI, I in the sober days of WWII. My aunt, cognitively disabled in traditional verbal and linguistic skills, learned to communicate in her own highly creative manner, and when I began to have serious trouble learning to read, write, and cipher, an unspoken fear arose that somehow I too was suffering from the learning difficulties that had afflicted my aunt. That fear was never dispelled and shadowed me through my school years, even challenging me to this day.

I also asked myself another question. Did my aunt's affliction only challenge me, or had others within the family also been scarred by her illness? Whether physically, emotionally, or mentally, I believe that the families of disabled children are rarely left untouched. Perhaps some individuals are more successful at adapting to their new life, but all are forever changed.

Physically I believe there were scars within my family. In the latter years of her life, my grandmother, the "Kristine" of the story, contracted leukemia, a blood cancer whose roots can be linked to chemical poisoning. Other family members battled heart disease, cancers, lead poisoning, and severe dementia. Could these illnesses all have had common roots? Did those tentacles of disease reach back through the years to the toxic Tiffany glasswork factory that polluted the Corona New York landscape and environment of my family's earliest years?

There are the emotional and mental afflictions too. The Willi character of my story was modeled after my mother. In real life, she was the primary caregiver for my aunt, but it caused her to lose her childhood. As an adult, my mother continued the role of caregiver for neighborhood children, grandchildren, and occasional seniors, but she never lost her yearning for those lost years of carefree play and abandon. The children she cared for during her life were the beneficiaries of that lost childhood, for she filled their lives with creating, discovery, and the joy of play.

My mother, active and always involved in learning for the 93 years she was given, evidenced two conflicting family traits: the first was that she carried her parent's embrace of unconditional love and acceptance forward to subsequent generations, though in private she'd pray about more than a few happenings. However, having embraced the faith of her father to sustain her, she battled the more sinister side of those formative years throughout her entire life. That dark side of life was fear; fear of the unknown and change, but most importantly a fear of not measuring up to the unconsciously imposed standards of her childhood.

With all those thoughts in my head, I committed to writing this book. If this story could document what daily life was like for my grandparents, if I could know them more intimately, perhaps I could understand the environment and times that allowed their lives to unfold as they did. The research tasks necessary for such a book took years with many false starts, the loss of important sources of information through death, and the uncovering of surprising new information.

To know the early years of my family's life, I engaged in extensive research that included heartfelt conversations and interviews with those who knew my grandparents best: my mother, her siblings, cousins, friends, and extended family. I pondered over journal pages kept by my mother, read an array of books, and searched endless magazine and newspaper articles about the social, medical, political, and religious viewpoints of this historical period, and mapped the genealogy of my family. While it was relatively easy to uncover the stories of my family's early years—including well documented and repeated quotes—it was almost impossible to get into their skin and know my grandparents' inner emotions, motivations, fears, or triumphs. Not unlike others of their generation, they kept those personal thoughts and feelings locked tightly within themselves. To understand them on this level, I had to stitch together all that was known about them, then reach into my own psyche and read my soul, for a part of them lives there still.

My real life aunt and uncle, the story characters of Sophie and William, were the primary reasons behind my grandparent's move from the city, but within days of arriving at their new home, the family's focus abruptly changed—now they simply had to survive. The home of their dreams had become a foreign land and every day challenged them differently.

The state laws of Connecticut affecting my epileptic aunt were different than those in New York. Now, the haunting threat of a possible incarceration for their daughter was gone and the fears that had followed the family's every move were magically disappearing. My grandparents could relax to some degree and let the real life Sophie develop in a more natural manner. The child responded in spades. My uncle, given more responsibility and allowed to be his own person became less troublesome. He developed a personality of his own that allowed his strong mechanical skills to be showcased, but he never lost his willful nature or the pushback that defined his early life.

The story of my family's *Hiding Place* and their unique daughter became a tale of change, courage, acceptance, and finally resilience. While at first survival was the daily norm, those obstacles were overcome and long-forgotten dreams began to re-emerge. My grandparents needed strength and vision as they met their future, and they found it in each other, their family, and their faith.

My grandmother's dream of a college education for her two oldest daughters became a reality, as did her dream that the *Hiding Place* home, complete with flowers, shrubs, lawns, and trees, would become a haven for family and visitors alike. She saw her son and daughters marry and her first three grandchildren born. The winds of life continued to blow for my family and their lives went on long after the conclusion of this telling. Sometimes their life winds were gentle breezes, but at other times, gales and storms railed with destructive power. So it is for each of us, the winds of life will always blow and each of us must find our way.

About the Author

Dorinda Lundin has been excited about writing for much of her life and has been successful at publishing a research-based article about her husband's Swedish heritage and a short story about sailing on Long Island Sound. After retiring from careers in the family custom framing business, education and teaching, she was able to devote time to more serious writing.

In this, her first published novel, Dorinda has given voice to the struggles of her grandparents, their family and the unique place they called home. She was especially moved by family stories about an aunt she never knew, her mother's sister who suffered from a strange disease the family called *Bubbles on the Brain*. Interested in history, genealogy, and family dynamics, Dorinda began to research the disease and the reasons behind the family's move from an urban entrepreneurial life to a primitive farm in rural Connecticut.

Dorinda and her husband live in Woodstock, Connecticut on the original small family farm her grandparents purchased in 1920.

Made in the USA
Middletown, DE
29 March 2017